T0334987

Field Research in Africa

Field Research in Africa

The Ethics of Researcher Vulnerabilities

Edited by
An Ansoms, Aymar Nyenyezi Bisoka,
and Susan Thomson

 JAMES CURREY

James Currey
is an imprint of
Boydell & Brewer Ltd
PO Box 9, Woodbridge
Suffolk IP12 3DF (GB)
www.jamescurrey.com
and of
Boydell & Brewer Inc.
668 Mt Hope Avenue
Rochester, NY 14620–2731 (US)
www.boydellandbrewer.com

© Contributors, 2021

First published in paperback 2021

All Rights Reserved. Except as permitted under current legislation
no part of this work may be photocopied, stored in a retrieval system,
published, performed in public, adapted, broadcast, transmitted,
recorded or reproduced in any form or by any means, without the
prior permission of the copyright owner

The publisher has no responsibility for the continued existence or accuracy
of URLs for external or third-party internet websites referred to in this book,
and does not guarantee that any content on such websites is, or will remain,
accurate or appropriate

British Library Cataloguing in Publication Data
A catalogue record for this book is available from the British Library

ISBN 978-1-84701-269-2 (James Currey paperback)

This publication is printed on acid-free paper

Printed and bound in Great Britain by
TJ Books Ltd, Padstow, Cornwall

Contents

Contributors

An Ansoms is Professor of Development Studies at the Université Catholique de Louvain in Belgium. She leads the Centre for Development Studies. Her research concerns the challenges of rural development and land conflicts in land-scarce, post-conflict environments. In Congo, her team's research focuses on natural resource conflicts. In Rwanda, she coordinates a research project on the role of civil society and local administration in agrarian and land policies. The team had extensive expertise on research ethics in conflict-prone environments.

Ghaliya N. Djelloul earned her PhD in Sociology at the Université Catholique de Louvain, Belgium. She is a member of the Centre for Interdisciplinary Research on Contemporary Islam (CISMOC) consortium. Her research interests lie at the intersection of gender studies, socio-anthropology of Islam and feminist sociology of space. Her research focuses on Islamic feminism in Belgium and on women's mobility in Algiers.

Elísio Macamo is Professor of African Studies and Director of the Centre for African Studies at the University of Basel in Switzerland. He is currently working on technological artefacts in African urban settings and is also interested in understanding the contribution which Area Studies can make to the disciplines. To this end, he has been reflecting on ways of conceptualising Africa which avoid the pitfall of representing the continent as a problem to be solved, but rather as an opportunity offered to social scientists to improve their theoretical, conceptual, and methodological tools. He regularly offers methodological workshops to African doctoral students on behalf of the Council for the Development of Social Science Research in Africa.

Emery Mushagalusa Mudinga is Director of the Angaza Institute, and a consultant based at the Institute for Rural Development Studies – ISDR Bukavu – DR Congo. He holds a PhD in Political and Social Sciences from the University of Louvain-la-Neuve and a master's degree in Development Studies. His research focuses on land grabs dynamics and peasant resistance in Africa; armed group dynamics and the politics of DDR in post-conflict zones; governance and natural resource conflicts; conflict transformation and peace-building; and the politics of research decolonisation and collaboration. Over the past 15 years, he has worked with several NGO and UN Agencies, governments and other institutions both in research, counselling, capacity development, and event organisation.

Aymar Nyenyezi Bisoka is an Assistant Professor at the University of Mons and researcher at Ghent University in Belgium. His research focuses on issues of access to natural resources, peasantry and armed groups and afro-critical perspective in social sciences. Nyenyezi Bisoka is involved in teaching and coordinating research-action projects in Belgium, Burundi, Democratic Republic of Congo, and Rwanda.

Susan Thomson is Associate Professor of Peace and Conflict Studies at Colgate University. She is the author of *Rwanda: From Genocide to Precarious Peace* (Yale University Press, 2018) and *Whispering Truth to Power: Everyday Resistance to Reconciliation in Post-Genocide Rwanda* (Wisconsin University Press, 2013).

Gino Vlavonou is the Programme Officer with the Conflict Prevention and Peace Forum at the Social Science Research Council, Brooklyn. He obtained his PhD from the School of Political Studies at the University of Ottawa. His dissertation focuses on discourses of autochthony in the Central African Republic. Vlavonou's research has appeared in *African Security*, *Revue Tiers Monde*, *African Identities*, and *Glocalism*. He has received scholarships and awards from various institutions, including the Canadian Social Sciences and Humanities Research Council.

Rosette Sifa Vuninga is a Centre for the Humanities and Social Sciences Research Council doctoral fellow at the University of the Western Cape's History Department in Cape Town, South Africa. Her PhD project focuses on ways in which ethnic and regional identities are experienced among the Congolese people of Cape Town. Vuninga's research is in the field of 'migrating violence' and explores issues related to the politics of identity and belonging.

Foreword: It is about Us

Elísio Macamo

O NE OF THE most appealing things about research is the cosy feeling it gives researchers that they are contributing to knowledge. The feeling is not misplaced. Indeed, research accomplishes a lot. Even if one were to be cynical and point out that not all research contributes to knowledge, it would still be possible to argue that not yet knowing is also knowledge because not knowing and knowing why we do not know is a form of knowledge. This is particularly the case when we carry out research in 'unfamiliar' contexts on delicate subjects. An 'unfamiliar' research context is not necessarily a culturally distant setting or a setting unknown to the researcher. Rather, it is a context within which researchers deploy the concepts of science in order to render the context intelligible.

Often, though, the impulse to know does not come from those settings. It comes from other scholars who assume that the importance of their work is acknowledged by all. To be sure, research is all about deploying concepts and theories to render the world intelligible. The issue, though, is whether rendering the world intelligible gives researchers an entitlement to know. In other words, knowledge production is not the outcome of a mandate given to researchers by those who are 'the subjects' of research, or the settings which are researched upon. The mandate is directly drawn from the commitment of the individual researcher to the very idea of rendering the world intelligible. There is, therefore, a sense in which research as the translation of the right to know is an ethical issue right from the beginning. The researcher claims the right to intrude into settings and people's lives in the service of some higher goal which might not be immediately relevant to the settings and the people about whose life the research will be spilling the beans. Researchers have successfully ignored this issue by appealing to the positivist idea underlying the pursuit of knowledge, namely the commitment to improving human welfare.

The problem with this positivist idea, as we know from the history of science – not least, the history of knowledge production under colonial and neo-colonial conditions – is that such a commitment has also been deployed alongside the goal of effecting changes in the way other people live. Such changes are to be affected without the consent of those who are the object of research. Every time, therefore, a researcher is in the field and goes about collecting data, the researcher is effectively engaging, at least theoretically, in an ethically problematic enterprise for the simple reason that the researcher is simultaneously claiming the right to change people's lives independently of whether the latter wants to change, or not.

Moreover, the presence of the researcher may unleash expectations which the researcher most certainly will not be able to meet. It is almost as if researchers were asking people to engage in an unfair bargain. Researchers secure their own livelihood by doing research and, in exchange, they hold out the promise of a better future to the people about whom they gather knowledge and who would like to see their livelihoods improve straight away. Sometimes, these ethical issues can come up during fieldwork. I have experienced that myself. Almost twenty years ago, I was conducting research in my country of origin, Mozambique, as part of a large-scale collaborative research programme at a German university where I was based at the same time.[1] I was doing research on how local communities cope with disasters, and hired students from a local university to help me interview members of the community. I made arrangements with the village authorities to visit the village on a Sunday and carry out interviews with volunteers. Upon arriving at the village centre, most of the villagers were assembled waiting for us. I asked each student to interview three individuals, but as soon as they started interviewing long queues formed in front of the six students aiding me.

When I pointed this out to the village authorities and remarked that students were not supposed to interview more than three individuals, they told me that this would not be possible because everyone expected to be interviewed. He warned us that it might be unwise for us to not meet their expectations. I insisted that we could only interview a few,

[1]   I published the results of this research project in Macamo 2017.

after which the village authorities advised us that – for reasons of safety – we should then say that our team would return the following day for further interviews. Since I had not planned to return and did not want to leave people with false hopes, I declined the suggestion. After having reached the assigned number of interviews, we stopped. The village authorities then grudgingly explained the situation to the villagers. Upon hearing the explanation, there was an uproar with many chanting that they too wanted to be 'written down'. This is a literal translation of the vernacular (Tsonga, a Bantu language), i.e. *ku baliwa*. It comes from the verb *ku bala* (to write), and it happens to share the same stem with the word 'forced labour', which is known as *xi-balu*. The link is not accidental, since people conscripted for labour had their names recorded on paper and underwent an interview. Fortunately, nothing particularly nasty happened, but later one village elder told me what the real issue was. I carried out my research in a region that had been badly hit by floods in the year 2000. An American non-governmental organisation (NGO) had conducted a survey shortly afterwards and six months later the NGO returned to the area and distributed food to those who had been interviewed.

What at first seemed to me like an unusually enthusiastic commitment to helping researchers collect data to produce knowledge turned out to be a particularly thorny ethical situation. Not only was I paid to do the job of researching that I was doing, but I was doing this on the back of people living in dire straits and who generously shared information with me. All I could offer them was the positivist promise of a 'world made better' by scientific knowledge. And from there I realised that I am not alone. Every time a researcher sits down with an informant, they are both locked into a nasty manipulative logic that transforms the researcher into an intellectual highwayman, preying on the innocent hopes of people who cannot defend themselves from the prying eyes of the global knowledge production conglomerate. Of course, researchers are not bad people and the overwhelming majority of them are full of good intentions. However, the context within which they go about their work, is lopsided and heavily loaded.

There are no words to describe how timely the book you are about to read is. An Ansoms, Aymar Nyenyezi Bisoka, and Susan Thomson – together with the contributors gathered in this fantastic volume on the ethics of research – offer us glimpses into the intricate ways in which being a researcher is really about losing one's innocence. This is not merely because of the very difficult moral dilemmas bearing on the subjects researched themselves, but also, and perhaps more significantly, because of how morally exacting it can be to be a conscientious researcher. And conscientious researchers are what the editors and contributors to the volume turn out to be. This manifests in the tensions, as the editors spell out in the introduction to the volume, embedded within reflexivity and positionality. More than simply gathering and analysing data, the research process is a deep ethical inquiry into our right to know, a right which was not given to us by those about whom we write, but rather by our own sense of intellectual entitlement.

Beyond the specific tools that researchers deploy in order to make sense of their data, this ethical dimension seems to be an unacknowledged part of the process of knowledge production. This is so because, deep down, knowledge production is not about 'them', i.e. those unfamiliar contexts and people. It is about 'us', i.e. those of us who describe ourselves as researchers and conduct our inquiries under the unspoken assumption that ours is a noble activity. No matter whether the people into whose lives we meddle have given consent – or fully understand what the scientifically defined forms of 'consent' mean – serve as evidence of whatever researchers want to claim and document. But then again, real scholarship is measured by the degree to which one summons enough courage to acknowledge this ethical dimension. An Ansoms, Aymar Nyenyezi Bisoka, and Susan Thomson, and each of the contributors to the volume, are real scholars. With this volume they are rendering the rest of us a timely and very good service. This is a book worth reading for the lesson in intellectual humility and ethical awareness it offers.

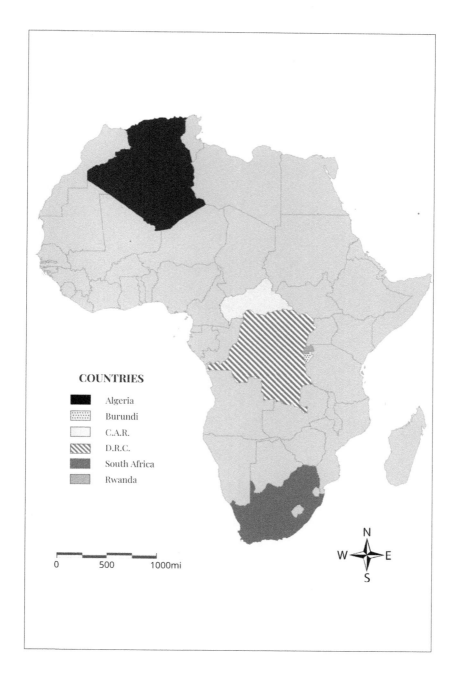

Map of Africa showing fields of research. (Sasha Mikus, 2020)

Introduction: Fields of Vision, Emotion as Reflexivity[1]

Susan Thomson, An Ansoms, and
Aymar Nyenyezi Bisoka

FIELD RESEARCH IS not what it used to be. Ethnographers, oral historians and other qualitative researchers committed to years-long fieldwork are engaged in a series of ethical and emotional compromises, from design, to write up, to publication. Field researchers juggle the demands of being a researcher and of being human – in balancing the recording of data with the emotional demands of listening to, of analysing and reporting on personal and often contradictory narratives in ways that meet and, ultimately, expand the disciplinary standards of 'the field' through publication. Each contributor to this book embraces the complex and contradictory humanity of those who participated in their research, as well as their own, as a matter of minimum ethical practice. Indeed, simply talking to people is a process fraught with multiple ethical and methodological concerns. These concerns matter all the more for those working in violent or conflict-affected locales (Campbell 2017; Cronin-Furman and Lake 2017; Perks and Thomson 1998; Thomson *et al.* 2013; Wali 2018).

---

[1] For their probing and thoughtful feedback, we thank Evan Schmidt, Rosette Sifa Vuninga, Tammy Wilks, and our anonymous reviewers.

The overarching theme of this book is how to balance the emotional effects of fieldwork – on the researched, researcher, assistants, intermediaries and gatekeepers, community members, and others – as a central element of ethical practice. After all, it is people who commit violence, experience violence, and who recover from its effects, as individuals and as members of local and national communities. The challenge is to recognise how, and in what ways, feelings differ from emotions, something each of the chapters that follow engage with in one way or another, with each author providing insights into how their emotions become part of the research process. Understanding emotion is a central element of a reflexive practice. Each of our authors unpack what many field researchers know, but rarely discuss openly – that building relationships, doing participant observation, generating field notes, and more – are products of emotional expressions, body language, and social dynamics. To turn these aspects of fieldwork into data requires an ability to understand and explain the wider sociopolitical context, in turn requiring the researcher to distinguish feeling from emotion, as part of their reflexive practice.

The foundation of a reflexive practice is the ability to recognise the emotional responses in ourselves and others, while distinguishing them from feelings. Emotions are the bodily and mental states that drive behaviour – anger, fear, affection, and humour, to name but a few. They are triggered by certain stimuli and are accompanied by behavioural changes, detectable in facial expressions, gestures, vocal timbre, trembling, skin colour, and so on. When a person experiencing these emotional changes becomes aware of them, they become feelings, in turn becoming conscious experiences to be documented, analysed, and evaluated. Feelings are internal subjective states that, generally speaking, are known only to those who have them. They are expressed through language; we learn about each other's feelings in narrating what we feel, often expressed as emotions. Yet, survivors of violence often lack the language they need to narrate their physical or emotional pain (Scarry 1985), adequately explain feelings of fear (Bourke 2006), or disclose the ways in which their memory triggers are sensorial, meaning sights, sounds, or smells can transport a victim back to the moment of harm (Coetzee 2019; Jethro 2020).

It is of ethical and methodological importance for researchers to remain mindful of assuming that we can truly know the emotional states of our interlocutors. We – whether researcher or researched, intermediary or community member – show our emotions, but we talk about feelings. Such recognition allows the researcher to more fully recognise how their emotions, and that of their interlocuters, are shaped by the wider sociopolitical context and hierarchies of power in order to better navigate ethical concerns when they arise, as the chapters in this book demonstrate. This means, as part of the researcher's reflexive practice, that we too must remain alert and attuned to reading facial expressions and body language, for those who participate in our research are doing the same of us, according to their own local categories and meanings.

The Politics of Publication

Each contributor to this book has struggled in one way or another to bridge the chasm between our public academic life and our private emotions. In many ways, we have each managed to work with limited institutional support for our mental health, as communities of care for those of us working in violent settings are limited (Theidon 2014). Where they do exist, it is often a product of the researcher taking the initiative with a handful of trusted confidantes. We confine ourselves to people we trust and care about, and who trust and care about us. However, the space for broader reflexivity around our inner anxieties as normal human responses to violence is limited and often undervalued or misunderstood as narcissistic by dissertation committees, editors, and the senior colleagues who hire and promote us. In advocating for the recognition of the human dimension of research, our reflexive-positionality dialectic illustrates that emotions can add to the rigour of the information gathered and the overall integrity of the research process by ensuring greater accountability for the claims and arguments made. This, in turn, gives editors, peer reviewers, dissertation advisors, and job search committees a chance to evaluate our findings with confidence. Finally, in a nod to the transparency we crave in the academy, we clarify the reciprocal co-mentoring relationships that underpin our book. An Ansoms worked most closely with Djelloul, Nyenyezi Bisoka, and Thomson; Aymar Nyenyezi Bisoka with Ansoms and Mudinga; and Susan Thomson with Vlavonou and Vuninga. Many of our authors sought additional feedback and engagement with their individual chapters, and these readers are acknowledged in the footnotes of the chapter in question. Each author also provides a list of additional readings at the end of each chapter, being a list of sources that have shaped their thinking.

Disciplinary norms of publication favour a completed evaluation and analysis. Ignored or downplayed is the process of being in the field, the searching, confusion, boredom, dead-ends, and inner-dialogue that precede publication. The Self is thus hidden in favour of academic authority. Yet, our analysis is a product of people's words, silences, body-language, histories, choices, place, politics, and more. Each interaction is imbued with the emotion of feeling, living, breathing, thinking humans, both positive and negative, heightened in many cases by the post-conflict or violent setting (Carpenter 2012; Chakravarty 2012; Lawther *et al.* 2019; Shesterinina 2018). Until recently, academic authors were to present themselves as neutral, or not to represent themselves at all. The norm of scholarly writing requires that the author is seen but not heard in the text; third-person and often-passive voice predominate, e.g. 'it was found', rather than the active and more honest, 'I found' or 'I experienced'. There has been in the last fifteen years or so a move away from a strictly neutral authorial voice, as journals and presses make space for the personal motivations and ethical choices of fieldwork (MacLean *et al.* 2019).

However, despite this promising progress, the reality remains that much of the discussion on the emotional anxieties, fears, empathy, anger, and guilt of personal experience of research, and their role in the production of knowledge, is relegated to prefaces or appendices of academic books or the 'notes' or 'reflections' sections of journals. Very few of these personal narratives are provided by researchers working at home, or from country or regional specialists with years-long, field-based relationships, or for activists or practitioners who also undertake research in sustained ways. All of these researchers have a wealth of practical, ethical and emotional experiences that differs in scope from the stereotypical foreign researcher whose presence predominates in the literature on fieldwork ethics in conflict settings (e.g. Cramer *et* al. 2011; Grimm *et al.* 2019; Mazurana *et al.* 2014; Nordstrom and Robben 1995; Smyth and Robinson 2001; Sriram *et al.* 2009. Cf. Akello 2012; Bouka 2015; Dery 2020).

The silence of the unsaid of research is further enhanced by something the Western academy culture of 'publish-or-perish' considers anathema. Academics are to publish within the hierarchy of scholarship (peer-reviewed books, articles, and chapters), teaching (textbooks) and service (blogs, media interviews). Publications for hiring, promotion, and tenure are valued in this order, with research published in 'prestigious' journals or presses garnering greater professional reward, at least in the Anglophone academy.[2] Publishing standards and norms conflict with more than the goals of the academic merit system, as scholarship favours technical language and disciplinary jargon, in turn restricting the scope for getting the perspective of the researched, the researcher, and the everyday sociopolitical context under study. Indeed, what counts as superior field research is often a product of dissertation supervisors, peer reviewers, or editors, who get to decide the scientific value of data produced. Implicit in this reality are assumptions about who can ask what kinds of questions, where, how, and with whom. Lost in these structural barriers is the push-and-pull of the internalised ideals of what it takes to get published and the emotional reality of long-term fieldwork.[3]

The demand of conforming to the publication metrics set by the market-oriented logic of publish-or-perish, whatever the personal cost, has two major consequences. First, it deprives the researcher of the much-needed time to consider issues of epistemology, method, and methodology, and it pushes researchers to ignore questions around the emotional vulnerabilities of the work. However, slowing down to consider issues of epistemology, method, and methodology – through a reflexive-positionality framework – is crucial (discussed more fully in our Conclusion). It is only in this way that the researcher can find the much-needed space for discussing what should be core to the research endeavour. What counts as knowledge in the social sciences? How can

---

[2]   We know that different institutions value publications differently, based on the teaching and advising expectations of faculty and of promotion and tenure processes. This insight is based on our own experiences in Belgium and the United States, as well as in our mentoring in Canada, Democratic Republic of Congo, Kenya, Namibia, Rwanda, and South Africa.

[3]   A note of caution. We do not advocate for the 'confessional' style of writing that some scholars publish about their fieldwork adventures. Researchers who write about the poor decisions they made during fieldwork as a way to absolve themselves of their wrongdoing, operate in this confessional vein. Such publications rarely practice reflexivity. Instead, the author admits to poor ethical decisions, writing to seek redemption from their colleagues for those decisions. Confessionals are dangerous because they often provide the validation the researchers require (publication), while downplaying or disregarding ethics training as part of one's preparation to undertake fieldwork. At the same time, confessional writing tends to consolidate the power imbalance between the researcher and researched, something we cannot condone. There are numerous examples of this kind of writing, none of which we cite.

we 'dis-orient' academic ways of knowing and doing? In which ways can we aim to not fix or essentialise either the researched and the researcher, or the time and place in which the research was carried out (Leonardo 2018; Said 2000; Smith 2012)? Our nod to time and space is crucial here, as we are fundamentally arguing that the researcher is an instrument of knowledge and, as such, the method we choose is both a technical and political choice. Our access to a particular field site, or our perspectives about the topic under study, may change over time. While more time can allow for deeper engagement with people and place – as we see in the chapters of Ansoms, Nyenyezi Bisoka, Vuninga, and Thomson – time can also heighten the emotional and social intensity of fieldwork as well as the expectations of 'home', whether narrowly or broadly defined, as Djelloul, Mudinga, and Vlavonou discuss in their respective chapters.

Second, it is crucial for the researcher to have the necessary space to question how emotional pain affects the demeanour of the researcher, both in the field and on the page. How does the violence that researchers witness or experience affect their analytical lenses and the way in which they interact with participants, colleagues, community members, and others, as well as the research environment? Our contribution to the debates is on emotional vulnerabilities in research, notably the particular challenges faced by African-born colleagues working in African field sites, whether at home or abroad. In addition, in writing in English our authors are working in their third or fourth language, which is no small feat. As such, we consciously chose, in consultation with authors, to produce an edited book, to allow contributors to express themselves with greater vulnerability than the peer-review process leading to a special issue of a journal might allow.

Lastly, in order to foreground the reflexive insights of our authors, we have placed in the concluding chapter the literature review and our interdisciplinary analysis of the methodological and practical debates that inform our book.

How We Have Organised the Book

Each chapter in our book is shaped by a willingness of each contributor to engage with the emotions that in turn make plain the messier bits and pieces of academic knowledge production. We start with the ideas of political scientist Gino Vlavonou of the University of Ottawa in Canada. He begins with a reflection on the difficulties of meeting the institutional requirements of gaining ethics clearance with the challenges of adhering to those guidelines on the ground. Vlavonou introduces the concept of 'skin connection' to demonstrate how the expectations of being a black African shaped his relationships with his home institution, his interlocutors and, ultimately, himself, as a young black man whose research interactions were shaped by gender norms and patriarchal expectations of young men like him. Vlavonou's chapter does more than identify the misfit between graduate-level research design and methodology courses and ethical practice in the field; it also reminds the reader that meeting the ethical requirements of one's institutional review board is rarely sufficient.

In the second chapter, Emery Mushagalusa Mudinga of the Higher Institute of Rural Development in the DRC examines the ethical and emotional demands of being an 'inside-insider', meaning someone who is of the place and people he studies. A political scientist by training, and a peace practitioner by profession, Mudinga teaches us how to manage the expectations of community members and the need to develop security protocols, especially when such concerns seem like second-nature. As someone of the place, who knows it so intimately, physically and emotionally, security is often assumed. Mudinga cautions against this, asking researchers who study 'at home' to take even more precautions than foreign researchers might be asked to do by the institutional review committees of their home institution. Ghaliya N. Djelloul, a sociologist at UCLouvain, takes the analysis of 'at home' a step further in the third chapter. She argues for researchers to commit to an ethical sensibility as central to an overall commitment to 'critical reflexivity'. In so doing, Djelloul reminds readers of the need to be able to understand and explain how identity is multi-situated, that is, as a product of identity but also how others perceive those identities as a 'mid-sider' (meaning neither research insider nor outsider). In Djelloul's case, she mediates between being an 'African' and being an 'European', even as she remains bound to gender, household, and community norms about how women should behave in places marked by explicit patriarchal social codes and expectations. In the end, Djelloul's chapter is a call to decolonise the Self through her tactic of acting the 'dutiful daughter' and strategically deploying 'pious lies' in the course of navigating her professional and personal lives at home in both Algeria and Europe.

In the fourth chapter, Rosette Sifa Vuninga, an oral historian at the University of Western Cape in South Africa, reflects on how she has navigated her status as an educated woman in the diasporic Congolese communities in Cape Town. Critically, Vuninga assesses her stance as a young Congolese woman who has also experienced xenophobia as well as the emotional and financial hardships of being a refugee in South Africa. Vuninga sees herself as an 'inbetweener', as she analyses her ability to ethically and practically document the lives of Congolese people living in Cape Town. In so doing, she walks the reader through almost a decade of qualitative research with people who are, in some cases, her friends and confidantes, to illustrate the ethical dilemmas of working with research subjects who are just like her. Vuninga, like Dejelloul and Vlavonou, also reflects frankly and plainly on the gendered and classed complications of research with those who view the researcher with a measure of suspicion and distrust. Along with Mudinga's concerns about physical and emotional security, Vuninga's chapter also reminds us that trust-based relationships are even harder for insiders to establish and maintain.

In the fifth chapter, lawyer and political scientist Aymar Nyenyezi Bisoka of the University of Mons and Ghent University, both in Belgium, in perhaps the most revealing essay of our book, digs deep into his emotional well to share how the murder of Sarah, a land-owning young woman he knew, shaped his sense of personal safety and security. Nyenyezi Bisoka walks the reader through the rollercoaster of emotions he did not fully anticipate, in part because of his commitment to his research on land conflicts in Burundi, Democratic Republic of Congo, and Rwanda, but also as a young black man from neighbouring DRC. In navigating his sense of immunity from the emotional and practical issues that befall foreign researchers, Nyenyezi Bisoka thought he, as a regional insider, would be able to manage the complexities of his research topic with the unspoken and subtle expectations of local political elites. In trying to scope out what had happened to Sarah, as evidence of local power relations, Nyenyezi Bisoka's chapter is a chilling reminder of the need to manage research relationships with participants, intermediaries, and local elites, both in the field and during write-up and dissemination.

In our sixth chapter, An Ansoms, a development economist at UCLouvain, examines the ethical and personal responsibilities of being a researcher and simply being a trustworthy human presence in the lives of her research participants. Writing about her twenty years of work in Rwanda, Ansoms reminds readers of the tricky and ethically fraught balancing act of needing to rely on the kindness, courtesy, and trust of others to not only conduct research but to connect as humans who have witnessed violence. In particular, Ansoms wonders about more than how trust is gained; she also draws us in to a conversation about how trust-based relationships evolve and morph over time and how they are shaped by the broader sociopolitical context.

In the final chapter, Susan Thomson, a peace and conflict studies scholar at Colgate University in the United States, introduces readers to her engagement with the concept of 'relational accountability'. She assesses and analyses her almost twenty-five years of research with Rwandans, first as a human rights lawyer and later as a scholar. Thomson demonstrates how she has struggled to honour the ways in which Rwandans themselves have wanted her to engage in politics in their country, even as her published works became political objects deployed to ends she sometimes found ethically unpalatable or difficult to understand. She argues for an ethic of dissemination, to mediate between what is expected of us when our findings take on resonance for audiences beyond the usual academic ones, and asks researchers to think of the politics and ethics of dissemination before fieldwork, not after.

Our collective field of vision is the thread that ties this edited book together. Each chapter asks the reader to think about the challenges and opportunities of embracing the role of emotion in the production of academic knowledge. We aim to expand the disciplinary fields of vision by offering multiple novel perspectives for researchers as they think through the design and conduct of fieldwork, as well as the publication of their findings. Each of the chapters that follow provide instructive insights for researchers to engage in a reflexive process of dissecting their feelings about an event, people, or place as part of emotional response to 'home'. Home is both a physical and psychic reality, as our contributors work in the place where they grew up, currently live, or conduct research within their diasporic communities. This reflexive response is what we mean by 'here and there', as referenced in the title of this introductory chapter. 'Here' is the physical location of the research, while 'there' is its emotional component that lingers during write-up and dissemination, acting as a memory trigger, as researchers recall the sights, smells, and sounds that inform the production of field notes, the writing up of our findings, and more as they interpret their fieldnotes and interview materials for publication.

Further Reading

Darling, Jonathon. 2014. 'Emotions, Encounters and Expectations: The Uncertain Ethics of "The Field"'. *Journal of Human Rights Practice* 6, no. 2: 201–12.

MacLean, Lauren Morris, Elliot Posner, Susan Thomson and Elisabeth Jean Wood. 2019. *Research Ethics and Human Subjects: A Reflexive Openness Approach* (February 12). American Political Science Association Organized Section for Qualitative and Multi-Method Research, Qualitative Transparency Deliberations, Working Group Final Reports, Report I.2. https://ssrn.com/abstract=3332887. Accessed 8 January 2020.

Smith, Linda Tuhiwai. 2012. *Decolonizing Methodologies: Research and Indigenous Peoples.* 2nd edition. London: Zed Books.

Sylvester, Christine. 2013. *War as Experience: Contributions from International Relations and Feminist Analysis.* New York: Routledge.

1

Skin Connections: Negotiating Institutional Ethics alongside Insider Identities[1]

Gino Vlavonou

FIELDWORK RAISES ETHICAL and practical challenges, all the more so in conflict or post-conflict settings. University-based ethics review boards in Canada and the United States are rarely attuned to the specific challenges and opportunities of conducting qualitative research with people living in these settings (Cronin-Furman and Lake 2018; Wood 2006). Some scholars treat ethical review as an institutional hurdle, even when the process helps prepare the researcher for 'the field' (Thomson 2013b). During field research, 'the responsibility to act ethically rests ultimately on the individual researcher' (Fujii 2012, 718. See also MacLean *et al.* 2019; Wood 2006). For some field-based researchers, there is data that 'simply cannot be accessed without an immeasurable degree of risk' (Kovats-Bernat 2002, 210).[2]

Researchers working in volatile and violent situations face risks but, of course, they are not of the same nature (Berry *et al.* 2017). As

[1] This research was supported by the Social Sciences and Humanities Research Council of Canada (SSHRC), and by the Economic and Social Research Council [ES/P008038/1]. I thank the editors for their incredible work.
[2] Others disagree on the basis that 'in no situation should a researcher risk his life or health to get the data' (Gallaher 2009, 139).

such, maintaining one's ethical sensibility is not always straightforward; indeed, maintaining one's ethical commitments is a process full of uncertainty (Hutchinson 2011). For instance, Nilan (2002), after a period of emotionally fraught fieldwork, wondered, 'whether it is [an] ethical practice to merely observe young people engaged in criminal and high-risk behaviour without warning them in any way, or notifying anyone about it. Or, indeed, whether it is ethical to eavesdrop on other people's private conversations, without letting them know you can understand what they are saying' (381). I faced similar issues. Informed consent, the safety of my research participants, and managing expectations of benefits are made more poignant by my presence in a volatile research site, as a young African man (in his early 30s), from Benin, working in Bangui, Central African Republic (CAR). I soon realised that my research process and maintenance of ethical practice was informed not only by my class standing but also by social codes and norms of masculinity. I argue that following ethical rules must be read according to researchers' identities. I do this showing how my skin connection and Africanity shaped my field research.

To explain how I managed my ethical commitments, to myself and my participants, I draw on my six months of fieldwork in CAR in 2017. I conducted my work in an environment characterised by open sectarian violence, which started in 2013 after Séléka rebels removed President François Bozizé. The rebels claim they represent the Muslim community, under the leadership of Michel Djotodia. A few months later, the anti-Balaka popular movement rose to fight the rebels.[3] The anti-Balaka claimed they represented the 'true Central African', in turn deploying hate filled rhetoric against Muslims. As such, my research question was set out to understand the meaning of indigeneity, to study what it means to belong, and why Muslims were targeted as non-citizens. My project concerns issues of discourse and meaning of 'Centrafricanity' (in French, *Centrafricaneté*, meaning being of CAR). I studied this from the perspective of political elites, rebel leaders, anti-Balaka leaders, as well as civil society actors and informal traders. Said differently, I wanted to understand how 'Centrafricanity' is generating sectarian

---

3   The anti-Balaka are a mix of vigilante groups, rural farmers, young unemployed, and former military officers who rose to fight the rebels. Although there were some Muslim fighters in their ranks, the majority were Christians, animists, and non-Muslim. Anti-Balaka attacked the Séléka and Muslims, forcing Michel Djotodia to resign. Since then, CAR has been searching for peace.

violence through the creation of an 'us-versus-them' dynamic as well as how the religious 'Other' is dehumanised. To probe such questions, my methodology involved semi-structured interviews, participant observation, focus groups, and studying the archives of the CAR's independent newspapers. I interviewed rebels, political leaders, and civil society actors (seventy-six interviewees for a total of ninety-two interviews). I also undertook fieldwork in Bangui (the capital city) and two other small towns in rural areas 225 km from Bangui (Yaloké and the mining village of Gaga).

At the outset of my research, I saw myself going 'home' elsewhere on the African continent. As a non-CAR citizen, I sought to work through my skin connection, my immediate visual characteristic. I relied on my 'Africanness', so to speak. Being from Benin, I had assumed that CAR could also be 'home'. In this chapter, I reflect on my approach to fieldwork as an African researching another African location. By 'reflection', I mean a 'sustained reflection on ethical research practices' (MacLean *et al.* 2019, 1). My analysis builds on this unevenness of being African in Africa. I probe the way my skin connection was perceived, how my own expectations shaped my field research work and how I ultimately built relationships, gained trust, managed my skin connection as well as power relations in fieldwork. I make visible how my identity shaped my encounters with the Institutional Review Board (IRB) during the field and in writing up my findings to complete my dissertation.

My chapter examines how ethical regulations intersect with researcher positionality. As the researcher is the instrument of qualitative data collection, it follows that the way each researcher deals with the rules must be seen according to one's positionality in the field. The first section of this chapter discusses how institutional ethics expectations shaped my entry to the field. Being aware of the ethical rules, I address issues that arose during the field and that were specific to my position as a junior scholar from the African diaspora studying another African country. From my research experience, researcher identity influences issues of access, trust, and power during fieldwork. I focus upon the challenges of navigating my identities to secure access and consent in the field. The second section delves into the details of my fieldwork as well as various situations where interviews did not always take place, despite my skin connection.

Practical and Ethical Conundrums with My Home Research Ethics Committee

Researchers have already exposed the ethical and emotional dilemmas they confronted in conflict zones (Wood 2006; Boumaza and Campana 2007; Nilan 2002; Buckley-Zistel 2007) but these dimensions must be put in conversation with their identities and the way the researchers position themselves during fieldwork, something which white or Caucasian researchers rarely do (although see Thomson in this book). Increasingly, African researchers have been writing reflexively about their situated knowledge and experience of fieldwork (Munthali 2001; Akello 2012; Bouka 2015; Yacob-Haliso 2019) but they have not always addressed practical ethical issues.[4] As an African working in an African country, but registered in a Canadian PhD programme, I must follow ethical guidelines (the *Tri-Council Policy Statement*) set out by my university in accordance with federal law. The formal legal elements of securing ethical approval rarely provide the researcher with the necessary tools to meet challenges that arise in the field. My chapter seeks to address this. My conundrum is that, as an African, participants anticipate me differently. This raises ethical challenges, particularly regarding access and consent during fieldwork. Specifically, various facets of my identity have shaped, facilitated, or hampered my capacity to build trust and gain access to the places and people I wanted to.

The IRB process is important but can preclude research in conflict zones (Bhattacharya 2014).[5] The IRB guidelines are not always suited for situations in difficult political settings (Bhattacharya 2014; Kovats-Bernat 2002), prompting other researchers to provide guidelines that could be specific to these difficult settings (Cronin-Furman and Lake 2018; Thomson 2009b). Moreover, 'collecting ethnographic data never takes place in an orderly context in which all ethical issues can be foreseen, and guaranteed through specific protocols' (Nilan 2002, 381). All researchers in conflict environments face risks and ethical dilemmas, meaning there is a growing body of knowledge about these dilemmas.

---

4   Recent African scholarship by black Africans demonstrated this importance of understanding one's positionality. See, for example, Githaiga (2016) and Wamai (2014) for Africans based at Western institutions and researching their home country; Bouka (2015) and Compaoré (2017) for researchers based at Western institutions and researching other African countries.

5   It can also preclude research in non-conflict zones (see Hemming 2009).

I cannot generalise the research context during my stay in the CAR, rather I sketch my experience to provide lessons for other researchers pursuing similar projects. All research projects in that sense must go through the ethics review board of each university. Behaving ethically rests on the researcher (Wood 2006; Fujii 2016) but some research contexts 'constitute permissive environments in which researchers can find themselves' (Cronin-Furman and Lake 2018, 5). Working in a permissive environment means that ethical challenges that arise often go undiscussed or, reporting – meaning the responsibility of meeting ethical commitments – falls solely on the researcher. I thus highlight a few of the challenges that arose and were specific to the violent context but also specific to my skin connection. Because of the nature of my project in a violent context, my ethics application received a full-board review and I was also asked to present my research and directly answer questions of the board members. I basically had to convince them that I could do the research and that I knew what I was getting into.[6]

Fieldwork seldomly goes as planned (Thomson 2009a). Mine was no exception. I had to provide evidence of local contacts to members of my IRB. Despite not having spent time in the CAR, I was able to get in touch with local contacts with the help of my thesis supervisor. However, in the time it took to process my application at the University of Ottawa, my local contacts left the CAR upon receiving promotions, a common occurrence among foreigners working in international organisations. Also, I was set to rent an apartment provided by a local NGO not far from downtown, in one of the safest places in the capital. When my institutional contacts left the country I no longer had a place to stay, a conundrum that formal IRB approval rarely considers. The local NGO did nothing to reassure me beyond confirming that I would have a place to live, in a pastor's house.[7] However, the same local NGO did host me and provided space for my work in its offices. Retrospectively, my encounter with the IRB prepared me for some dilemmas I did not face, even as I anticipated them. For instance, the IRB wanted me to 'investigate the affiliations (political or otherwise) of the NGO with which (the researcher) will be affiliated'. As part of that, I anticipated that the NGO would get to shape who I consulted and how. However, during the course of my fieldwork, my local partner was entirely hands-off. And, contrary to the advice of my IRB committee, I found the

---

[6]   Other researchers have had similar encounters with their IRB when researching in so-called difficult settings (see Thomson 2013b).

[7]   Whose name I cannot disclose, for I promised confidentiality.

CAR government did not directly interfere with my research. In fact, the government does not request academics to obtain any particular authorisation for conducting research. Nonetheless, my encounter with the IRB forced me to think about those issues prior to my departure and these were useful. It is better to be overprepared than not.

The researcher is not in full control of his environment nor the interview process. Emotional and physical risk can emerge at any time. The IRB is usually more concerned with the vulnerability of participants, assuming the researcher is in a position of power. I also did not work with local assistants which others have employed to help them navigate security and trust issues (Jenkins 2012; Kovats-Bernat 2002). For instance, Kovats-Bernat (2002, 214) used 'localized ethics' in his research where he 'took stock of the good advice and recommendations of the local population in deciding what conversations (and silences) were important'. The researcher's power in the field could depend on the participants. The researcher has authority during the writing phase and should uphold the 'do no harm' principle in order not to retaliate against elites who belittle them during fieldwork. This could be a principle when the researcher is the weaker party.

I was raised in Benin. My family could be considered middle-class and I grew up with my siblings and cousins in a middle-class neighbourhood in Porto-Novo, the capital. My siblings and I went to a private Catholic school. After my *license* degree (diploma earned after three years of university study), I moved to Canada in my early twenties. Canada was an option because I had a family connection in Quebec City. I was interested in development studies mainly because of the economic situation of Benin. It pushed me to undertake development studies at Laval University, although it is my later work with a think tank in Nairobi, Kenya that led me into conflict studies in the CAR. These early experiences inform my academic interest in CAR and in conflict. As such, I grappled with many faces of my identities when trying to conform to ethical rules for the conduct of my research. As feminist scholars have long known, one's identities shape and inform one's positionality, which in turn shaped my choice of field site and methodology (England 1994). I relate my experience for other researchers with similar characteristics to help them anticipate and mitigate their encounter with ethical rules and their institutional ethical review board requirements.

By positionality, I subscribe to Rose's (1997, 308) interpretation when she argues that 'facets of the self – [...] as well as aspects of social identity – are articulated as "positions" in a multidimensional geography of power relations.' Researchers have long understood positionality in terms of how various identity attributes influence their fieldwork. Madge (1993, 295), when discussing the politics and ethics of Western researchers, argues that 'a researcher's positionality (in terms of race, nationality, age, gender, social and economic status, sexuality) may influence the "data" collected and thus the information that becomes encoded as "knowledge".' Specifically, my positionality as a young black African man from Benin and based at a Canadian university resulted in ethical issues of trust, access, and anonymity. Positionality and identity have been used interchangeably and the goal in feminist literature was to target the situatedness of knowledge. I find this useful to probe ethical encounters that I faced in the field. It offers a lens with which I can consider various facets of myself against the information I have been given in the field. As fieldwork research carries ethical concerns 'every step of the way' (Cramer, *et al.* 2011, 2) I expose some moments of uncertain ethics and reflect on them.

In the Field

Consent

In my institutional ethics application, I requested, and was given approval for oral rather than written consent.[8] Beyond blackness, Africanity played a role in my consent procedure; more than skin connection, people at times saw a kin connection. For colleagues with personal attributes similar to that of their informants, it might be worth paying attention to the moment one seeks consent. Participants did not expect me to be engaged in procedural behaviour about consent at any level. Very few of my interviewees expected so, and some were confused by my discussion of, and asking for, 'consent' as understood by institutional IRB guidelines. This is related to how I introduced myself and greeted people more powerful than me. For example, political elites would start our conversation by saying 'welcome my son' or rather focus on *'jeune homme'* (young man) and would at times extend greetings to knowing how my family members

---

[8]   I chose oral consent for two reasons: first, issues of informed written consent are difficult to manage in violent settings because interviewees are afraid to sign any document and researchers know that. Second, due to the diversity of the interviewed population, I expected that I would encounter a wide spectrum of literacy skills.

(in Benin) were doing. They saw my skin connection as important. I fitted into local codes, as a young black man, from their point of view. Some elites did not take me seriously in the beginning and thus did not expect me to engage in such formalities. Consent was often seen as an unnecessary formality. During the field research, I would present myself and the research, and many times, they would already have started talking before I asked for consent.[9]

As something other researchers can learn from, it seems that not being taken seriously, mixed with how my African connection was perceived, created an atmosphere of cosiness and informality. It was helpful to gain trust as people already agreed to be interviewed. For instance, I used this informality to get individuals to talk to me even if it meant spending too many minutes discussing my family in Benin. It can be useful to ignore the expected formality of Canadian ethics. Researchers must trust themselves, and their knowledge of the local situation and how people like to interact to build good relationships. Ultimately, following the ethical commitments I had with my institutional IRB, I waited until the end of the interview to politely ask for 'consent' and present issues of risks and how they wanted me to anonymise what they said. One can wonder if this is still a valid request as the interview has already happened. But, consider how uncomfortable it can be to disrespect an elder by asking for consent. What I had to modify was the moment at which I would ask for consent. I used this with political elites most of the time. I consider this to have been an effective strategy since various important people I met were more interested in demonstrating the breadth of their knowledge to the young African newbie. Oral consent allowed me to remove a layer of formality and further signalled that I fitted into local norms.

With my non-political elites and interviewees in rural areas, I sought to gain trust with the same strategy: removing any layer that formality could put between us, such as the signing of a written consent form. Moreover, it could be associated with colonial power.[10] The formal side would have put me into the category of foreign or Western researchers

---

9   Other young foreign PhD researchers had similar experiences. For instance, some of Vorrath's (2013, 66) interviews with Burundian political elites involved 'a lecture on the history of certain aspects of Burundian politics' or even monologues that completely disrupted her interviews. She does not make explicit how the consent process unfolded.

10 Norman (2009, 73) has been declined interviews in Palestine for similar reasons.

in a context where the perception of nefarious foreigners is already acute. What I point to is a way to deal with power relationships in fieldwork in terms of access in trust.[11] For instance, a white researcher, Jourdan (2013, 21) notes that relationships are a 'product of unequal power relationship embodied by Africans, which have shaped the history of the continent'. As a young black man, I sought to dissociate myself from that representation because I always presented myself as coming from a Western institution and needed people to not see me as a black man behaving like whites. From fellow Africans, this is interpreted as a sign of deculturation, of being 'too foreign'. Hence, for my African peers, you must be aware of the level of formality you introduce into your relationships, to manage the emotional distance it creates between you and your interviewees. This is how I understood the issue of consent and used it to create and maintain trust. I present this for other black Africans to gauge whether it could be useful as a research strategy for them. I am not disputing the question of consent; this is an all-time and necessary requirement. In my case, by changing the *when* of the consent, I was able to build rapport and trust. The bigger issue could be related to the *how* and *when* to ask for consent.

In fact, CAR citizens have an expression for people in the category of black folks behaving like whites: *munju voko*, meaning black-skinned white or foreigners. So, my skin connection made me fit neatly into that category. One can find similar phrases in other African countries. In Senegal, for instance they use the word '*bounty*' to refer to someone black on the outside and white inside. As Ochonu (2019) notes, 'racial denialism runs deep' in Africa and its 'most poignant manifestation is in the widespread culture of social deference to expatriates with lighter skin tones'. As I suggest, ethical commitments must be read according to how the researchers' identity fits into emergent inter- and intra-African debates. For example, my failure to access some political elites made me realise that my skin connection, let alone my other identity attributes, were not enough to establish trust and access. I often realised that the same political elites who denied me interviews would grant them to foreign white researchers and journalists. Probably these elites did not see me as competent or they disregarded such competence because of my skin connection. I will probably never know.

---

[11] From the various encounters I share throughout this chapter, I did not feel I held much power over my interviewees. Of course, at the writing stage, power ultimately resides with the researchers as they are the ones who erase or make available certain information.

Failure to get access shapes what information I get and what I construct as knowledge. Current debates around the inclusion of global South scholars into the social sciences should also consider the racial aspect of gaining access to interviewees and building trust with them.

In terms of access to the people from whom I wanted to learn, my skin connection barred me from penetrating Bangui's 'good intention crew' as Lombard (2016) calls them. The 'good intention crew' are foreign humanitarian aid workers and international civil servants. During my field research, it was difficult to reach out to international NGOs, to ask for interviews. None of those I wrote to, to request an interview, followed-up, even when I was introduced by local members of the NGO's managing staff. My sense is that expatriates, as foreigners living in CAR, anticipate me quite differently. Probably because there was no interest in talking to, or learning from, a young black African guy, or maybe they were also too busy to spend an hour with a young researcher. My Canadian residency status was not enough. For instance, there is no visible attribute to my Canadian-ness. At the same time, one cannot build trust without access to the people. For African colleagues who will have to navigate this, my skin connection constrained my capacity to access internationals. For instance, I only managed to travel outside Bangui with the help of a CAR religious organisation after I had tried several times with an international NGO. My various attempts to travel with the UN mission were also unsuccessful. I had made a formal request for travel that has been 'stuck' in the administrative channel despite my multiple follow-up inquiries.

Impartiality, Empathy, and My 'Going Native' Experience

As a researcher, it is essential to maintain a sympathetic embeddedness in the locality, while at the same time ensuring a degree of professional detachment as appropriate to the context. Methodologically, empathy/sympathy is still the rule while doing fieldwork; it allows 'access to the logic and sense-world of persons' (de Sardan 2015, 36). de Sardan (*ibid.*) however, maintains that a real dilemma is combining empathy and distance. Moreover, embedding oneself is influenced by socio-economic class, financial capacity and personal attributes such as skin colour and nationality, as I discussed in the previous section. It is in my attempt to be sympathetic and embed myself that the on-duty and off-duty also becomes blurred.

My limited budget forced me to live a particular class of Central African experience. There was a silver lining, as living on the outskirts of town brought me into direct contact with the hate and resentment aimed at my Muslim neighbours. Being 'off-duty' or having some free time was almost impossible. Empathy/sympathy should remain a rule for every researcher to consider. This principle is complicated by researchers' individual identities, as well as the local relationships we develop in the field. My skin connection did not allow me to remain emotionally distant because I was perceived to be automatically an ally, empathetic and understanding of such discourses. Here, my Christian upbringing mattered because of the sectarian sensitivity of the conflict. Many locals advised me not to wear my African fabrics that look like Muslim attire. As I lived with the local family, I wondered if it was ethical to eavesdrop on their conversation? Or what to do with the information they willingly shared while we were having dinner together? Was I supposed to tell them not to share anything with me? This might be one of the possible ways to get a lived experience during fieldwork and one might have to live with the ethical dilemmas it brings around trust and consent. The situation was perfect for off-script discourse and gaining a general sense of how people felt. In that sense, preoccupation with how to 'do no harm' sharpened. Similarly, as I sought to dissociate myself from being perceived as white, I must be aware of how I judge what is harmful or not and not reproduce the assumption that Kovats-Bernat (2002, 214; Wood 2013) stated about the 'implied [...] intrinsic power relationship that conjures the colonial legacy of anthropology – one in which the anthropologist is assumed to be able to control or at least mediate or negotiate danger away from those with whom she or he is working'.

As an African who wanted my skin connection to matter, I relied on shared characteristics with the people around me, as I benefited from their advice around security. This example illustrates the point made in the previous paragraph quite well. As I was perceived as a 'son', for instance, both my host and the director of the local NGO instructed me to call and let them know where I was every time or if I got home late. On one instance, my phone died, I reached home later than usual and both men lectured me seriously about my irresponsible behaviour.

Fieldwork can change the researcher in unexpected ways and being emotionally close to the people you want to understand can quicken the process. I realised that in the CAR popular discourse, Central African and Muslim were addressed separately in the same sentence. Toward the end of my research period, I began using the same distinction. I reproduced the same divisions I was set to understand and deconstruct, and I felt uncomfortable with that. I still do not know how to escape the division implied in the discourse. For instance, Cohn (1987) unexpectedly changed her speech while researching defence intellectuals. As she immersed herself into their world, she ended up speaking like them. My interviews were smoother as I adopted the same rhetorical separation of Central African and Muslim and it became natural. In that sense, I could no longer maintain professional distance from the fieldwork. How I ensure it does not transcribe into my writing, remains a question that I grapple with. Ethically, being impartial was all but simple. Nothing in my ethics preparation or field research trip could have prepared me for these dilemmas. Most likely, being impartial is not realistic for any field researcher especially in a polarised and armed conflict environment. However, my responsibility is to not reproduce the dichotomies I have been socialised in during fieldwork.

Being a Spy[12]

Researchers employing ethnographic methods sometimes report that they faced accusations of spying. Not only does this raise concerns around access and trust, it also introduces an air of suspicion to the research process. Following the example of Fujii's (2014) 'accidental ethnography', the specific moment I relate below revealed how my identities intensified issues of power during field research.[13] I was not directly accused of being a spy but the situation in which the encounter happened was emotionally risky for me. Ethical research suggests being transparent and avoiding deception (with limited exceptions). This is a blurred area at times (Vorrath 2013, 67). So, in entering the field, I always faced a dilemma about how I should present myself in order to secure access to interviews. I could not say I was a Canadian researcher because I was not. Saying I was from Benin raised questions about why I was coming from Canada? So, I always had to

---

[12] Researchers are usually accused of spying in volatile security and political situations. It is context dependent and can also be dependent on the current international affairs. Jenkins (2012, 56) was accused of spying for the International Criminal Court (ICC) while researching in Kenya. Even a Kenyan national, but from a Western-based institution, faced similar accusations while in the field (Wamai 2014).

[13] Serendipity is another conceptualisation; see Ryan and Lőrinc 2016; Keikelame 2018.

emphasise my Beninese origin plus my student/researcher status in Canada as well as my relative youthfulness.

In August 2017, after knocking on doors at the National Assembly, I obtained the telephone number of Alfred Yekatom. He is a former anti-Balaka fighter who managed to be elected as a member of Parliament. Rambo was his nickname.[14] Interviewing an anti-Balaka commander was a crucial part of my research, especially as they were the one who spread the 'true central African' discourse. After several delays, he agreed to meet with me one Sunday. Our scheduled meeting for 9.00am finally took place at 11.00am. As I arrived at our agreed meeting place, a small restaurant, Rambo is surrounded by several young men, three if my memory serves, and everyone is eating. Rambo buys me a drink and asks me to sit down. I reiterated the purpose of my visit; he took the time to finish what he was eating and then he replies that he does not feel at ease speaking in public. Quickly, without notice, he asks me to enter his car (an old Toyota Rav 4) with the three other men. They explicitly wanted me to sit in the middle of the rear seats so that I was between two men. On the spot, it occurred to me that this was not a safe situation, but I entered into the car. After all, I wanted the interview. His driver started the car and we were heading toward an unknown destination. I had asked where to, but no clear answer was given. I was unsure of what to do. If anything was to happen, I surmised, then it would have already happened. After twenty minutes of driving with the driver constantly looking in the rear-view mirror, we arrived in the town of Bimbo. I knew this because I saw it on a road sign. Because the driver looked into the side mirrors, I assumed that he was checking if he was being followed. He then stopped the car and another guy started questioning me again about the purpose of my visit when I had already stated it was to interview an MP as part of my dissertation research.[15] After all that, the elected member then asked me to call him back in a few days. We never met again. So, the interview did not happen.

Reliving this unplanned moment made me realise how powerful individuals have a complete disregard for a young black foreign African man like me. Moreover, there are a few former anti-Balaka who turned

---

[14] He was arrested in October 2018 and transferred to the International Criminal Court.

[15] This situation happened in public administration as well. For instance, in order to follow the official procedures for meeting with the director of one public institution, other public servants had to 'question' the true purpose of my research.

and became MPs. So, an important question for me was to understand if his election was a reward for violence. Did the mobilisation of a 'true Central African' identity play a role? For my research, it meant certain information was just inaccessible because of my person. I came to that conclusion because Yekatom offered interviews and appeared in videos with war reporters and even on the France24 television channel. One possibility could be that I was not worthy of being given an interview whether or not I came from Benin and a Canadian university. African researchers' access to some information is complicated at times by our incapacity to escape the power relations we find ourselves in. I could simply not access Yekatom, even when he was a few metres away. This is also an example of how people make sense of researchers in general, of how they interpret our presence in their lives. The kind of behaviour someone deems applicable to a researcher reveals the position they have assigned to them. Since situations like these are unpredictable, a variety of factors can make the researcher needy and powerless and put him into danger.

Between Institutional Ethics and Some African Norms

During the course of my research, several participants felt the need to give me money for a taxi, to buy credit for my phone, or just because it was a festive day. I was struck by the fact that even when presenting myself as based in a Western university, some people gave me money. Most of those people were political elites, priests, and rebels, all the people who I perceived as more socially powerful than me. As a student with no income, it is fair to assume that the elites had more money than I do. At the same time, in several African societies, it is cultur- ally accepted for a patron to give money to show his status, and being young and African probably signalled that I fitted within such cultural codes. Gaining access and building trust meant that as a young African black male, I had to accept the money even if I did not need it. I think some African peers can recognise this gesture. As I navigated the issue, I think it might be useful not to refuse the proposed money (depend- ing on the amount) right away. Norms around deference to elders or just people who are older are important and must not be overlooked by researchers. Remaining attuned to these social norms demonstrates a level of local embeddedness which is important for gaining access and building trust with participants, particularly those who are more powerful. Accepting these small amounts was a sign of respect that I showed, and it made people willing to help me. I did not feel that political elites were currying favour as they did not make any direct or indirect comment about how to treat them in my research. This act reveals the position to which I was assigned: probably someone in financial need or someone who had not yet attained financial autonomy or adulthood. Accepting the money helped to build trust, especially when I had to meet the same interviewees several times. Showing that I respected their position proved to be useful. Refusing on the spot could have affected my efforts to properly build my snowball sample. Moreover, refusing could signal that I did not recognise their status, their authority, or could be interpreted as me behaving like a white or foreign researcher.

I had not foreseen, when securing my institutional ethics approval, that I would have fitted such African codes of deference and respect. I expected it to matter more that I came from a Western institution and considered the act of giving money as a conflict of interest because Canadian norms say I should not exchange money to get interview data. I felt uncomfortable accepting but did accept their token sums to build trust and gain access. At the same time, a female researcher who receives money might be seen differently in such a context, so I acknowledge the gendered dimension of this act: receiving money from interviewees as a young man. This was not a bribe but usually, a practice of social exchange in some African settings. A patron, someone in authority, proves his place by giving money to his clients. I was exposed to this practice as I grew up in Benin without ever questioning it. So, the context of the research, and my awareness about the role of money gifts, made the difference. As it is possible to find the same gesture in other African countries, this is about power and domination. These people were demonstrating their authority and financial capacity to a young man. The challenge here is that Canadian norms speak of conflict of interest when rather it is regarded as a demonstration of power in some African settings. Moreover, I cannot underestimate the influence of my upbringing in Benin. My parents were inflexible on respect for authority and elders and the impossibility of defying or questioning them. It played a role in the sense that as a young African man I felt compelled to defer to political and religious elites in CAR even if their behaviour frustrated me.

There have been instances when people of lesser economic income wanted various forms of assistance from me. This also presented a challenge in terms of gaining access and managing relationships in the field. For instance, I sometimes tried to use my Canadian-ness in specific settings to gain better access to interviewees. In one instance, a mayor of a district in Bangui took my Canadian residency seriously. It was a lady and she unequivocally asked to be paid before granting me an interview. That day, I had presented myself as a Beninese student researcher from a Canadian university. But it was my Canadian-ness that caught her attention. She responded that I was working for my interest and that she had no interest in sitting and giving me information. I then asked how much she wanted to be paid and she replied, 'You know, you cannot give 10,000 FCFA [approximately US$20] to a high-ranking authority like me.' My explanations of why I wanted to speak with her did not help me secure an interview and I left. It is all right to be denied interviews; this is a normal part of the research process. But researchers must be attuned to the how and why of interview denials, for such 'failures' can also result in useful information. The ethical challenge here was that my Canadian status was supposed to lead to financial outcomes. Clearly, I have no control over the skin-folk attributes that my interviewees deem relevant to them. On the one hand, others saw me as a 'son' without financial autonomy. On the other hand, pecuniary expectation came with my Canadianness even if I did nothing different to elicit that interest. In part, because researchers in fragile situations rely on various NGOs to conduct their research, confusion can result when members of these organisations expect payment (Cronin-Furman and Lake 2018, 3). I was not affiliated with an international NGO, but there was often an expectation of financial reward. This was another moment of 'accidental ethnography'. Moreover, she wanted to be paid for giving information and that is ethically also controversial. So, I sided with the option of not paying.

My research design also included speaking with rural inhabitants to understand whether the claim of being 'true Central African' meant anything to them. Indeed, several prominent anti-Balaka fighters came from rural areas. As I travelled outside Bangui to Yaloké, I needed someone to assist me because people's level of fluency in French was lower. My assistant understood quite well my foreign-based status. Hence, he wanted various forms of assistance. This was different from my encounter with elites in Bangui. He wanted me to help him travel to Benin, to meet with my parents, and to help him acquire bursaries to study abroad. In that rural area, expectations were not monetary, they were social. For instance, I met a group of internally displaced Fulani who suffered from the war. I had been touched by their stories but when discussing with the head of the internally displaced Fulani in the city, he wanted my writing to 'produce cows' for them.[16] As herders, the only thing they wanted was cows, but he knew that a young researcher could not buy them cows. Similarly, I have met anti-Balaka fighters in the area who did not expect money from me. They were interested in having a connection to a Beninese. For them, Benin *voodoo* is a powerful social force, and they expected me to help them increase their invisible power in order to resist the next Séléka invasion. The point is that in rural areas as well as with non-elites I have not been given money and I have not been denied interviews. My skin connection with them was relevant as they felt they could trust me because of my Beninese origin and the fact that I could understand some discourses about the invisible world (*voodoo*). Contrasting that experience to what has been said in the literature shows that my identity played a role. The situations researchers encounter and the ethical issues around access and trust are connected to their positionality.

Concluding Remarks

Fragile settings, armed conflict situations, and other broadly difficult settings constitute 'permissive environments' for unethical research (Cronin-Furman and Lake 2018, 5). Several challenges that relate to the context of the field can prevent the research from following the ethical rules and sometimes make it impossible. There is a growing consensus that only the researcher in those settings can set the limits of what is ethical or not (MacLean *et al.* 2019; Wood 2006). However, if the responsibility is ultimately with the researcher, how can he read and set the rules whilst taking into account his identities? In this chapter I have discussed how my identities influenced my approach to ethical conduct regarding consent and access during fieldwork. To do so, I introduced the concept of skin connection.

As a young black Beninese man based at a Canadian institution and studying another African country, I have paid attention to some of the ethical challenges that arose during my fieldwork. I have discussed how some elements of ethics cannot be foreseen prior to fieldwork and when the encounter with the IRB can be fruitful in raising awareness

---

[16] As Jok (2013, 157) noticed in South Sudan, for instance, 'frequent assessment missions do not necessarily yield aid' but, this interviewee specified writing. I had made clear that I was not affiliated with a particular organisation, but he still expected something. In my understanding, this is a way for him to use all the resources he can for the benefit of his people.

and in overpreparing for the possibility of government interference. On the one hand, some of the challenges were related to the difficult settings in which field research takes place and in that sense, do not set me apart from the experiences that other researchers encountered during their field research. On the other hand, other challenges were related to how, as a black African man, I fit into the local norms of my research context. Taking into account the gender dimension, this chapter provides a reflection on research by Africans who are based at Western institutions and study African countries that are not their country of birth.

Reflecting on these challenges brings an African perspective into discussion about ethics during field research, whilst considering how positionality and identity attributes relate to ethics. Moreover, the cultural norms of a patriarchal society are not the only ones that shape ethical choices on the ground. African scholars, whether of the diaspora or not, should reflect on the societal norms of the field. This chapter is a contributing step in that direction.

Further Reading

Chilisa, Bagele. 2012. *Indigenous Research Methodologies.* Thousand Oaks, CA: Sage.

Fujii, Lee Ann. 2017. *Interviewing in Social Science Research: A Relational Approach.* New York: Routledge.

Pierre, Jemima. 2013. *The Predicament of Blackness: Postcolonial Ghana and the Politics of Race.* Chicago and London: University of Chicago Press.

Schwartz-Shea, Peregrine and Dvora Yanow. 2012. *Interpretive Research Design: Concepts and Processes.* New York: Routledge.

2

Conducting Sensitive Research 'At Home': A Matter of Responsibility

Emery Mushagalusa Mudinga

A CADEMIC LITERATURE OFFERS a wealth of examples of how to collect data (Duschesne and Haegel 2008; Grawitz 2000). It also offers examples of how to put research participants at ease and of how to engage in knowledge construction based on data collected on the ground (Beaud and Weber 2003; Sanford 2006; Quivy and Van Campenhoudt 2011). We find examples of how to care for the researcher's security and for that of their collaborators (Ansoms 2012; Davidson 2004), and how to ensure the anonymity of the research participants (Ansoms 2012; Davidson 2004; Fujii 2010; Sluka 1995). However, very little is written on the ethical challenges embedded in doing research on 'sensitive' topics in a 'sensitive environment', involving 'sensitive' actors. Yamuna Sangarasivam (2001, 95), explaining the way she had to conduct research in a conflict-affected environment, says: 'Nothing in my academic training prepared me for the methodological challenges I faced while conducting fieldwork in a setting of war. No graduate seminar had schooled me in "methods in the field of battle;" no workshop offered "techniques for researchers, terrorists and native Others".'

More researchers have begun to carry out their work in settings in which they risk their own lives as well as those of their collaborators and of their research participants (Sriram *et al.* 2009; Thomson *et al.* 2013). Researchers are asked to improvise on how to work, live and survive in such environments while ensuring that their research is successfully conducted by the researchers' own standard. Because of the context in which it takes place, research in conflictual settings rarely bears no consequences. In some countries, the state itself represents a threat to the work of the researcher, especially when the topic appears dangerous to the eye of the state. I am referring here to government elites sitting at high levels of the state machine. In his work *Les Risques du Métier. Trois Décennies comme Chercheur-Acteur au Rwanda et au Burundi*, Filip Reyntjens (2009, 5) goes over three decades of research work during which he was constantly on the receiving end of 'political pressure from state actors'. Susan Thomson (2009a, 108; 2011) recounts having been placed in a re-education facility by the Rwandan government so that she could better understand what is and is not permitted when conducting research in Rwanda.

Researchers may be threatened by individual local actors, such as local elites, who think the research may conflict with their political or economic interests. Researchers may also be threatened by collective actors, such as armed groups, by specific socio-economic groups, and by ideological and political structures (Chatzifotiou 2000). Threats often derive from a situation of general insecurity, from 'cultural stereotypes' to 'social distance' between the researchers and the research subjects (Adenaike 1996, 6; Ansoms 2012, 3–4; McCurdy 1996, 52). These types of threats appear throughout the phases of the research process – from the collection of data to their publication – and can persist after the results are published (Thomson *et al.* 2013).

While all researchers may be exposed to the dangers of violent environments, the situation is more complex for local researchers who are also *insiders* of the context of their research. For them, research may not only cause harm to the researchers, their collaborators, and research participants; it also risks endangering the lives of their families and friends, even when these are not directly involved in the work. In this sense, physical threats are imminent, have another scope than for in-and-out researchers, and evolve in a different time frame. When can the researchers consider themselves safe from danger? When the threats stop? Should they avoid research topics that risk exposing them? Should they treat their research topics differently?

This chapter sheds light on understanding the challenges of research on sensitive topics in the researcher's own home environment. How to reduce the risk of causing harm to themselves, to the researchers' networks, to their inner circle, and to their professional lives? I would like to put forward the idea that regardless of the choice of methodology or bureaucratic safeguards, nothing can replace the personal capacity and ethical sensibility of a researcher to manage risks in the field. While bureaucratic tools and strategies may be important in the research process, researchers must rely on their personal attitude and skills in adapting to the context and in finding appropriate solutions for different scenarios.

In order to make this point, the article brings together reflections and anecdotal evidence from my own lived experience of research in my home country, the Democratic Republic of Congo. First, I highlight the utility of building personal networks in South Kivu, a violent research context characterised by on-going civil war and regional militia activity. Second, I show the importance of producing a security protocol, which should contain information on the practical developments of the research plan while allowing for reflecting on one's positionality during each stage of the fieldwork. Such planning invites the researcher to consider their positionality and emotional vulnerability in the field well in advance, to prepare for inevitable challenges. Third, I discuss the importance of thoroughly considering how to introduce oneself and one's research topic to people in the field. Finally, I address the issue of publication and dissemination strategies, arguing against the rapid publication of research results. Ultimately, I question the naïve idea that all results should be published or even made publicly available. Such considerations are of importance both for the *insider* and the *outsider* researcher. However, throughout this chapter, I will show why local researchers are more exposed to certain ethical challenges than their foreign counterparts. The overall ideas in my chapter are based on more than eight years of professional experience in the Eastern Democratic Republic of the Congo (DRC), a country that has been marked by violent conflicts since the 1990s. The examples cited in this chapter are mostly drawn from a particular field trip carried out for my doctoral degree in South Kivu in 2012.

Sensitivity, Opportunity, and Network-Building at Home

My research focuses on land grabbing by local elites in the territory of Kalehe, South Kivu, in the Eastern part of the DRC. This is one of the most insecure regions in Congo, marked by a long history of ethnic conflicts linked to the presence of armed groups. Ethnic conflicts have contributed to the deterioration of the relations between different communities and have also enhanced suspicion and mistrust within communities. Conflicts often revolve around securing access to or control over natural resources. Local elites are important actors in these conflicts, drawing legitimacy from their political, economic, social, or military power to grab land. To focus one's research upon such conflict is to expose oneself, as the research will unavoidably touch upon the interests of powerful actors. Nevertheless, as a native of the area, and inspired by more than three years of professional NGO experience in community conflict resolution, I saw my research as a way to bring about change at the local level.

However, despite my ambition to make my research contribute to better living conditions for poor people at the local level, I was not naïve. Some locally powerful actors saw my research as a danger to their economic interests while others saw it as an opportunity to understand land tenure dynamics and to unveil the identities of the 'land-grabbers'. Anecdotal evidence from my initial experiences in the field will serve to highlight both the importance of respecting locally embedded ethical rules and the primary role of the researcher's personal responsibility. It will also, and importantly, bring to the forefront the importance of the preparatory phase, as well as the idea that threats in the field are unpredictable, constant, and specific according to whether the researcher is an insider or an outsider. In the following paragraphs I will present a few stories in which I faced challenges, dilemmas, and threats, both individually and as part of a team.

The Importance of Networks in Dangerous Contexts

In order to frame my experiences, I employ the concept of a network as a starting point. A network is defined as 'a collection of concrete individuals who are members of different systems of unified categories' (Mitchell 1973, 21). According to Borgatti and Halgin (2011, 2), it constitutes 'a set of actors or nodes along with a set of ties of a specified type (such as friendship) that link them'. Along the same lines, Kapferrer (1973, 84) states that 'in a network, individuals are either directly or indirectly linked to a benefit or an interest which becomes their focus'. For Kapferrer, as for other authors, connections amongst individuals may be formal or informal and are often based on strategic alliances within social structures (Eisenhardt and Schoonhoven 1996; Granovetter 1985; Powell *et al.* 1996; Uzzi 1996). Without opposing these perspectives, Bourdieu highlights the importance of social capital to explain the functioning of networks within social structures. Social capital 'is not what you know but who you know', which is defined by

Bourdieu as 'the sum of an individual's or a group's real or fictional resources which result from having a more or less institutionalized network of relationships including contacts and mutual recognition' (Bourdieu and Wacquant 1992, 119; Gauntlett 2011, 2). It can thus be concluded that in social structures, networks play a role in the production and dissemination of information. They allow its members to make decisions or to avoid dangers. A social network is, in this sense, a mechanism that allows for the protection of its members. Owen-Smith and Powell (2004) support this idea by showing that networks play three important roles: they are a source and a channel for information; they signal and confirm status; and they have a role in the production of social influence and authority.

However, even when a researcher is inserted into locally embedded social networks and has strong links with other nodes (members) of the network, he is not safe from ethical risks and cannot take the success of the research for granted. An anecdote from a research trip in 2011 in Numbi, a small village on the highlands of Kalehe, illustrates my point. My team and I were investigating land conflicts between the local Hutu and Tutsi populations and their relations with the local indigenous populations. The conflicts revolved around land grabbing in the context of the return of Tutsi refugees. Our research strategy included individual and focus group interviews. For the latter, we had planned to first conduct focus groups that were ethnically homogenous, then move to focus groups with actors of different socio-economic categories. We had already taken the time to explain our methodology to the local authorities (the *chef de poste d'encadrement administratif* and the chief of police) in the presence of an agent from the intelligence service.

Local authorities, for their part, had not expressed any concerns. Notwithstanding, as soon as our first two interviews with a couple of leaders from the Hutu community were completed, the intelligence service agent told us that he wanted to be present for each of our interviews and that this was a necessary condition for us to continue the research. I replied that our research did not represent a risk and that this was well known by his superiors. I added that in order to respect the ethical safeguards of our research, I would rather halt the research than give in to his requests. Needless to say, stuck in an isolated area far away from the nearest city, without phone coverage or roads, and being aware of the dangerousness of the intelligence services, my colleague and I spent an uneasy night. Early in the morning we learnt that the intelligence agent had made a three-hour-long march to reach the closest telephone booth. He had called his superiors based in the local city of Kalehe. To my surprise, the agent's superiors told him that they knew me and that the work I was conducting did not present a danger, highlighting its importance in terms of conflict resolution. As a consequence, the agent let us work without any further interference. His superiors were acquainted with me because of my previous experience in conflict-transformation work. In my previous work for a local organisation, I had already established a good working relationship with them, and I had involved them in the peace-building process at the local level. Had I not known those men I do not want to imagine what could have happened to us.

A similar situation occurred during my second trip to a mining site named Koweit, in the rural city of Nyabibwe. In Koweit, we were denied access to the site by local miners who were members of opposing mining cooperatives. Although we had explained the aims of our research on the previous day, they forbad us in a very harsh tone to conduct interviews and to take pictures on the site. Because my colleague is a *muzungu* (white person), their line of inquiry was even harder. They were convinced that all white people coming to the mining site had a hidden agenda, which potentially made me suspect as an individual who might 'betray our country'. After about an hour of unsuccessful negotiations, I decided to phone a local authority with whom I had worked in the past and who was acquainted with the nature of my research. The authority instructed the locals to let us conduct the research. However, his orders angered them, leading to even more frustration. Eventually, even though we were allowed to carry on with the research, we were aware of the threat embedded within the miners' frustration. In the evening, we contacted a couple of them; we shared a drink and we tried to clarify the misunderstanding. Eventually, some of them became key informants. However, in alternative cases, such situations are often too complex to be solved with a drink. Researchers working in sensible environments are often faced with these sorts of obstacles and must learn to be creative and to come up with sustainable strategies to face them.

Both examples show how my existing networks helped me to navigate research relationships, allowing me to continue with my research. On the other hand, having access to a network should not be an excuse for researchers to underestimate the physical or emotional risks they might encounter. Furthermore, in certain places, as in the aforementioned case of Numbi, it is impossible to communicate with one's network because of the lack of roads, telephone, or security conditions. Researchers must learn to adapt and have the capacity to continuously reconsider strategic decisions in relation to ethical challenges. A context analysis and a security protocol (developed further below) are important tools in order to explicitly make the researcher think about the risks involved. The protocol also allows the researcher's network to sound the alarm in case of problems.

Before Fieldwork: Elaborating a Security Protocol

Preparation before departure for the field is always important before moving to areas beset by conflict. However, whereas ethical review boards mostly concentrate on the risks involved for the research participants, relatively less explicit reflection is invited around the security of the researcher and their research collaborators. Moreover, after initial approval has been given, ethical review boards have limited control over what happens throughout the research project. In this case, risk assessment has to be made for the duration of the project. As Sluka (1995, 227) highlights, 'dangers can be managed through precaution, planning and the researcher's ability to manoeuvre'.

In line with Sluka, I propose that the researcher's security is a matter of continuous reflection. And such reflection can be facilitated and structured by elaborating a security protocol. This tool helps to push the researcher to make the risks they face more explicit and to think about possible challenges and solutions. Moreover, the protocol can also provide third parties with a technical tool that informs them about the researcher's movements in the area of work, in order to intervene more efficiently in case of problems. Meyer (2007, 59–61) engages with this reflection in what he conceptualises as Decision-Making strategies. Elaborating this idea further, I propose a security protocol including the following items:

- The letterhead and logo of the home university or institutional affiliation of the researcher;
- The name of the researcher and his collaborators (if any), including all their personal information;
- A security focal point (name and information): this is a person appointed by the researcher and responsible for following their movements and reaching out to any other contact (local partners or colleagues) in case of need. The focal point could be a family member, a colleague, or a collaborator. They should be able to manage difficult situations and have the capacity to reach out to relevant contacts in case of problems. It is

convenient to choose a security focal point from amongst local and trusted collaborators. For example, having a focal point in Belgium when the work is being carried out in the DRC would not be as effective;

- The objectives of the research;
- A description of the context of the research area, including physical security and emotional risk details. This description should include a risk analysis of possible dangers and the likeliness that they will happen (high, moderate, low);
- A detailed schedule of research: a table including the geographical location, the number of days and the dates at which the researcher will be at each location (with map or GPS locations if possible);
- Itinerary: the itinerary followed by the researcher. Important locations should be highlighted (i.e. towns, park/forest, important centre);
- The presence of important institutions in the researcher's area: police posts, army bases, hospitals. These may provide reference points that can be contacted in case of need;
- Important security phone numbers: supervisors, colleagues, family, security services, journalists, human rights organisations, embassies, and so on;
- Evacuation points in case of danger: airports, roads or points of passage, neighbouring countries;
- A medical kit: the researcher should indicate whether they consider carrying one;
- A charged telephone and, when possible, some emergency batteries and credit for airtime. The researcher should try to be reachable even in areas without phone coverage. Inability to communicate may alarm colleagues and supervisors who are following the researcher's movements. The researcher should specify when they will communicate with the focal point, and which protocol the focal point should follow if contact cannot be established;
- A description of the accommodation: the researcher should state where they are staying. They should also choose accommodation that allows them to avoid security risks as much as possible. Depending upon the context, the researcher may have to change their accommodation. This should be communicated to the security focal point;

- Lastly, the signature of the researcher and, if possible, of the security focal point should appear on permission letters and so on.

These elements are essential, but they remain flexible. As Meyer (2007, 59) puts it: '[r]isk will never be planned out of research; but using personal experience and substantive literature to develop decision-making strategies for institutions and lone researchers can help better manage risk.'

A security protocol can play a preventive role and may avoid loss of time by specifying how to circulate information in case of need, in order to promptly reach the appropriate persons. Establishing a security protocol also invites the researcher to explicitly think about 'strategies [that] take into account power dynamics and choices available to actors in a particular setting' (Meyer 2007, 59). However, it should not be considered as a panacea for all potential problems. The researcher's own sense of responsibility is the most important factor in risk management, together with their capacity to improvise and adapt. The next section illustrates how remaining open-minded to change is crucial once entering the field and begins right from the start when introducing oneself in the field.

In the Field: Introducing Oneself and the Research Topic

When engaging in research in a conflict-affected context, the way in which the researcher introduces themselves and their sensitive research topic may represent a first obstacle. Key informants – also those met during the early 'preparatory' stages of the research – will assume that the researcher has a nefarious agenda, often right from the start. An erroneous introduction into the field may result in the refusal to work with the researcher or may allow actors to position themselves in relation to the presence of the researcher for their own benefit. Moreover, the introduction of a research topic may bring up unexpected tensions. Denzin (2009, 72) mentions how the existence of 'multiple truths' can lead to 'truth intolerance' or 'truth shock and counter-shock' when the research topic is introduced. I experienced this situation in 2009.

I was just starting participatory action research on land and interethnic conflicts in Kalehe territory (in the North of South Kivu province) for the organisation *Action pour la Paix et la Concorde* (APC). With a colleague, we undertook preliminary meetings with different ethnic groups. During a focus group with Hutu participants in Nyabibwe, we explained the goals of our project, the way in which we would conduct our research, and the expected outcomes. During our presentation, the attitude started to change and small paper leaflets began to circulate in the room. We were countered with increasingly aggressive questions about our legitimacy to work on interethnic conflicts. We both started to feel very awkward. I managed to send a message to the driver, asking him to come closer to our location with the car (for physical security reasons). The research participants asked us to show them documents of all kinds. They accused us of working for the government, suggesting that we were using the cover of 'independent researcher' for some hidden agenda. It was one of the hardest moments of my research life.

What I learnt during those circumstances is to not give in to panic. My colleague and I answered the questions clearly and diplomatically. We also talked about our own limits as researchers and explained that, as members of a non-governmental organisation, we aimed to understand the situation and to produce recommendations that came from the local community. At a certain point, I proposed to take a break and share a soda. This helped to de-escalate the crisis. The experience also illustrated the importance of creating space for reflection in interaction with other team members and for adjusting the research strategy. We used the break time to inform our superiors of the problems we were facing and redefined our questionnaire guide in case the focus group would continue. Eventually, we were able to reassure the group of our intentions. The attitude of the research participants in this brief anecdote is a challenge that occurs more often – particularly in conflict-prone settings. In most cases, research participants are not trying to stop the research but to protect themselves. The researcher must be transparent and make sure that the 'interviewees feel safe' in order to obtain their collaboration (Ansoms 2012, 3–4).

Moreover, in the introduction of very sensitive topics, the researcher must walk a thin line between being honest and open on the one hand and diplomatic and strategic on the other. Brown (2009, 213) shows that for local participants, the researcher is also an object of research: 'A variety of individuals is consistently trying to gather information on us.' Therefore, the topic of the research must be introduced to the participants while taking into account the local sensitivities of the context; that challenge may be further complicated by the various interest groups that are approached in the research process. The language that the researcher adopts should be tailored for the actors with whom they are interacting, notably the authorities who are in charge of validating mission documents, the research teams on the ground, militias or regular army forces, and peasants or elites. When presenting their research, the researcher should take account of the fact that these actors do not all follow the same rationale. For instance, instead of talking of 'land grabbing by local elites in Kalehe' to those elites, I speak of 'the challenges in elites' contribution to local development in Kalehe'. Little by little, I introduce more precise issues dealing with conflicts related to land grabbing, while taking care to approach them within the broader and less politically charged topic of local development. It is up to the researcher to be inventive and aware of what is practically and ethically possible.

Sluka (2009, 283) highlights that 'it is crucial that the researcher tries his best to counter the false perceptions of his work by the public so as to avoid being grossly misunderstood or interpreted'. When I was working on local land conflicts and ethnic cohabitation in South Kivu, certain local actors started claiming that we had received funding to legitimise the foreign ownership of land in the Kivu. For others, our work was a pro-Rwandese operation. Only slowly and through a long process of building trust were people able to understand our work and its usefulness for transforming local conflicts.

At the same time, it is always possible that things might go wrong. In such a context, an outsider researcher may find his access to the field blocked (see Reyntjens 2009; Thomson 2009a). Consequently, they might be jailed or placed under house arrest. However, an insider researcher may face even more serious consequences, affecting themselves or their family. Besides the danger of imprisonment and torture, their public reputation might be stained far beyond the research arena. Therefore, the researcher, both insider and outsider, should try to evaluate their relationship with thier research environment in the short, medium and long term – for themselves, but also for their collaborators. This vigilance is necessary not only during the introduction phase but also during the writing and the dissemination period.

During and After: Thinking Through Publication and Dissemination Strategies

Should results be disseminated or not? If yes, how, why, and to whom? Any research endeavour should serve to inform, educate, and produce scientific knowledge of interest. How useful is a study if it cannot be published and be made available? Why should a researcher invest money and energy in a research that only results in the 'graduation' of the researcher and that is not of service to society at large? More questions may be added. As such, I plead in favour of a cautious approach when it comes to publishing research results. As academic researchers working in sensitive contexts, we must avoid publishing results on sensitive topics under pressure, and we must pay attention to the consequences that sharing our documents may have. It is important to keep in mind that readers that are politically motivated and moved by their own agenda may (at times deliberately) misinterpret our writings, our style, our quotes, or analysis, and may use them to harm others. A high level of caution is needed for the local researcher for whom the threat is permanent given his relations with the local milieu and its actors. Just publishing in the name of 'truth' and for the sake of information can – under certain conditions – be very problematic.

A first major issue to consider when entering the publication phase is to properly anonymise the research data. While participants in any situation, as human beings, deserve the protection of ethical standards, individuals working and living in situations of armed conflict, of state repression, and of serious human rights violations are clearly and specifically more vulnerable. This is even truer for those individuals who are not outsiders but belong to the society that is the object of the research, and thus are obliged to stay in the region as political and social actors, as researchers, or in any other function (Sriram 2009, 58). In sensitive and violent contexts, future access to the fieldsite depends on a measure of self-censorship. Certain information may hinge on the ability to access the field in the future or it could endanger the lives of the participants. Sriram (2009, 59–61) tells how one of her key participants was assassinated by the Liberation Tigers of Tamil Eelam (LTTE), a radical armed group engaged in a process of constitutional reform with the government. The armed group was the topic of Sriram's research and Dr Triuchelvam (the main participant) was a member of parliament and took up an active part of the peace process. Dr Triuchelvam had not yet finished reading the draft sent to him by Sriram when he was killed in a suicide bomb attack (a common LTTE tactic at the time). Sriram (2009, 66–67) concluded that researchers should be aware of what their research can cause in terms of targeting people. Ideological or extremist groups that see in the research a possible threat to their interests may target respondents and key informants. Some people may be killed to prevent them from revealing some truths.[1]

---

[1]   Sriram does not directly link the assassination of Dr Triuchelvam to her research. She said the doctor was already a targeted person as a prominent person in civil society and very critical of the LTTE. However, Sriram considers

Second, the publication phase may also confront the researcher with the ethical dilemma of how to frame the position of key actors involved in the research. This is particularly challenging for individuals who have an ambivalent status within a given society, those who are at the same time charismatic and cruel. This was the case during a research trip with my team in Kapapa (fake name for the purpose of this paper), in the territory of Kalehe. One of the village leaders, I will call him Jeff, was one of the key proponents in a mining conflict that involved two opposing cooperatives. The conflict had resulted in the loss of human lives on several occasions.

It should be noted that during our encounters, Jeff had always shown great respect towards our research team. He had listened to us, offered us drinks, and always had time to talk. Moreover, the rhetoric of other people in the local setting around Jeff's position was generally positive. Multiple individuals in Kapapa were aware of the key role that Jeff had played in the expansion of their city. People described him as someone with an entrepreneurial spirit, creative and protective, and as some interviewees put it, 'he [Jeff] welcomed everyone. You could obtain a parcel of land on credit and pay it later' (unnamed landless peasant participants, interview). Even those working in Jeff's plantations, especially women, described the working conditions as better than those provided by other local plantation holders. For example, it was possible to rent one hectare (instead of a quarter of a hectare elsewhere) in exchange for a day of work in Jeff's own plantation (*salongo*) while elsewhere more work was required. Jeff allowed for payment in instalments, while in other plantations only full payments were possible.

However, a few local actors were more critical and suggested that people were concealing the truth out of fear of being expelled from the plantation. The further we moved away from Kapapa, the more critical our participants became of Jeff's positionality. Some accused him of working for a foreign country (Rwanda), of being 'selfish' and 'a dictator.' For a researcher, each of these statements, regardless of their origin, speaks of metadata (meaning data that can be understood from movement, rumours, body language, and so on) that are important to refine our analysis of conflicts and of an actor's positionality (Fujii 2010). That is why we took such statements into account. Our analysis of a first

---

that both his status (civil society critical activist, key person in the negotiation process) and his encounters with people researching on the LTTE could have a probable link with his assassination (Sriram 2009, 60–61)

round of research data resulted in the publication of an article that was very critical of Jeff's position in the conflict, and of his relationships with military and armed groups. The article showed that, as with many other local elites, Jeff was using power, financial means, and acquaintances to instrumentalise local conflicts and to marginalise the people involved.

However, a second round of field research confronted us with particular challenges. This time, while discussing with Jeff, he asked us what we had done with the results of the previous research phase: 'I never saw the publications that followed our first exchanges, may I have a copy of it?' Additionally, in the absence of any visible tangible outcome, he rightfully wondered what the purpose of our research was: 'You say you are conducting research, but what the impact will be on local development?' (Jeff, interview). We were seriously challenged by these questions. We refrained from telling him that we would send him the article that followed our first exchanges, as we were aware that doing so would have meant the end of our research in Kapapa. We told him that the final results would come with the publication of my doctoral thesis and that our work would assist decision-makers and development practitioners in the elaboration of their programmes. Eventually, we decided to not immediately publish the article online. This allowed us to gain some time and to define other strategies for sharing our results with particularly sensitive participants.

The aim of this section is not to question the utility or necessity of publishing research results. Publication remains the main means of communication for a researcher. However, caution is also necessary during the post-fieldwork phases. The researcher should evaluate the consequences that may follow if publications fall into the wrong hands or in the case of untimely online publication – particularly when working in sensitive contexts. It is important to avoid sharing drafts prematurely, or to publish too rapidly without fully taking the time to consider the possible consequences. This is particularly challenging for junior researchers, who often struggle with publication pressure in order to gain legitimacy in the professional academic world. In some cases, it may be better to deprive science of some information, rather than causing harm to research participants or the researcher themselves.

Conclusion

This chapter explored the challenges that I faced, working individually and in a team, in the conflict-prone setting of eastern DRC. I highlighted that regardless of all preparation before entering the field, the researcher's on-the-spot ability to assess difficult situations remains key in order to put in place effective strategies to deal with the challenges encountered. However, decent preparation may help to sharpen that ability; for example, by collecting information on the context, by analysing the risks before leaving for the field, and by developing strategies to introduce the research and the researchers. Preparing a researcher's security protocol is crucial as well, given the unpredictability of the field. The researcher remains the only individual responsible for decision-making and for finding solutions to problems, given that he is the only person capable of assessing their severity. However, the elaboration of a security protocol invites the researcher to explicitly think of the risks in advance and to foresee a back-up in case of problems.

Furthermore, in conflict areas where formal security services are lacking or where they are controlled by criminal and corrupt actors, the support of a strong local network composed of political, administrative, security, and civil actors is key. Sharing a drink, a bottle of wine, or paying for someone's airtime in order to allow them to communicate with you may be crucial. Some researchers do not approve of these methods. However, being able to interact with those who are aware of the changes in the local context can reveal aspects that might someday be crucial to the researcher, to their security, and to the security of the research participants. Building and maintaining a network has a price and requires adaptation.

Finally, my chapter suggests caution during the publication phase (as does Thomson in this volume). Being prudent in sharing preliminary drafts and in spreading publications online may be key in maintaining accessibility, but also in protecting the researcher's own security. The publication pressure is particularly challenging for junior researchers working on their own setting. Researchers are, on the one hand, pushed to publish rapidly in order to gain professional legitimacy. On the other hand, they may underestimate the long-term impact of publishing certain findings, analyses, or conclusions upon their own lives or that of their family.

Indeed, however challenging it may be to do research in conflict-prone settings, these challenges are even more pronounced for those researchers working in their own environment where they live or work together with their family. The researcher should be aware of the effects of their research on those close to them in the short, medium and long term. Upholding ethical principles and attention to avoiding any harm should be part of the researcher's culture, together with the awareness that their own sake and that of their participants are more important than the research.

The examples used in this chapter come from my experience as an academic and activist researcher. It is important to mention that research in conflict zones is complex and sometimes it can be difficult to give with precision, what are the best ways to prevent or tackle obstacles. Dealing with ethical challenges is, and will always be, a matter of responsibility. Researchers must be aware of their vulnerability when engaging in conflict-prone environments.

Further Reading

Buckley-Zistel, Susanne. 2007. 'Ethnographic Research after Violent Conflicts: Personal Reflections on Dilemmas and Challenges'. *Journal of Peace, Development and Security* 10: 1–9.

Sluka, J.A. 2015. 'Managing Danger in Fieldwork with Perpetrators of Political Violence and State Terror'. *Conflict and Society* 1: 109–24.

Sriram, C.L. 2009. 'Maintenance of Standards of Protection During Write up and Publication'. In *Surviving Field Research: Working in Violent and Difficult Situations,* edited by C.L. Sriram, J.C. King, J.A. Mertus, O. Martin-Ortega, and J. Herman, 56–68. New York: Routledge.

3

A Gendered Research Journey: Ethical Dilemmas of an Algerian Immigrant Recovering the Memory of 'Home'[1]

Ghaliya N. Djelloul

RESEARCH, AS A socially mediated process, is a socio-cognitive experience where ethical questions are intertwined with the production and interpretation of data (Gaudet and Robert 2018; Sabourin 1997). Thus, ethics are constantly navigated alongside epistemological, methodological, and theoretical paths (Genard and Roca i Escoda 2014; Maunier 2017). Yet, when research is socially located at the crossroads of one's personal and professional lives, ethical protocols become a type of autoethnography (Butz and Besio 2009, 1660). This practice of self-representation was first defined by Reed-Danahay (1997, 9) as a 'form of self-narrative that places the *self* within a social context', in order to trace both the effects of social mediation on the knowledge produced, and on 'our constitution as researching subjects' through them. Such critical (or doubled) reflexivity, as an 'identity-work' being

[1] I am grateful to my colleagues Naïma el Makrini, Joachim Ben Yacoub, An Ansoms, and the two anonymous reviewers of this chapter. Their empathy and benevolence enlightened my reflection and allowed me to move forward on the path of reflexivity.

done 'self-consciously', may bring us to a transcultural moment, articulated in relation to oneself and the wider social field that includes an
audience of 'others'. This puts the agents of signification (academics)
and its objects (research subjects) as opposite poles on a continuum.
Butz and Besio (2009, 1660), who share the common use of subjectivity as an epistemological resource, describe five types of autoeth-
nographies that represent a variety of 'self-representational' practices
in which authors 'cross, straddle, or inhabit the boundary between
non-academic and academic subject positionings'.

Throughout my chapter, I define critical reflexivity as a 'self-critical
sympathetic introspection and the self-conscious analytical scrutiny of
the self as researcher' (England 1994, 82). This framing helps me locate
the contradictions in my identity that occurred as I navigated different forms of social mediation during my research on women's spatial
mobility in my native suburbs of Algiers. Returning to a 'home' that my
family and I had left seventeen years earlier, fieldwork as a process has
triggered for me a continuous subjective movement between myself
and my 'double', both as an individual and as a researcher (Mbembe
2013).[2] Therefore, critical reflexivity helped me understand how my
multi-situated position has evolved, as new social mediations occurred,
finally breaking out as a 'travelling identity' of a transcultural subject
(Mbembe 2013, 145). It is thus crucial to consider how this specific
experience has shed new light on ethical dilemmas, as new social mediations occurred. Following Pratt's (1994) understanding of a transcultural, reflexive research subject, and imagining fieldwork as a site where
transculturation occurs, I argue that ethics need to be contextualised as
we progress through the social relations tied to the scientific journey,
and should be guiding principles rather than a set of rigid norms (Faës
2014). In reflecting on the conflicts I have encountered between my
personal morals and the ethical principles of research while struggling
to conduct fieldwork, I demonstrate that my situated ethical perspective is always directly tied to my positionality (Bouka 2015; Mullings
1999). I thus analyse how I am 'situated in relation to the people and

[2]   Borrowing this expression from Mbembe (2013, 177), the image of the 'splitting in two' of the Self (creating its doubles) reflects on 'time' and its 'con-
catenation' as a matrix of structuration of subjectivity through memory,
remembrance and other modalities of presence of the past. Intimately mixing rational and dreamlike consciousness, time is only experienced though
listening to the body's sensations, which can be multiple.

worlds' I am studying, 'and to the fields of power that constitute those relationships (Butz and Besio 2009, 1666).

To this end, I elaborate on three constituent stages of ethical dilemmas. In the first, *pre-fieldwork* stage, I acknowledge how my personal and activists background explain how different components of my identity (such as gender, class, and ethnicity) shaped my positionality (as a mid-sider that embodies both a 'dutiful daughter' and an 'immigrant') when entering the field. In my *fieldwork* stage, I explain the reasons that led me to start my research under cover, as I faced a physically constraining and emotionally intense gendered experience of containment in the subordinated position of 'young girl' in domestic spaces.[3] This leads me to explain why I later used the cover of 'dutiful daughter' to reach out to other women, and examine its costs in terms of ethics. Finally, *post-fieldwork*, I consider how a political dimension that only emerged after the process of socialisation, by sharing the space, time, and language, has produced a movement between my 'Self' and my 'doubles', and made me recover my memory, namely, the responsibility of 'representation' when thinking and writing about Africa from its diaspora and having to face multiple audiences (Manning 2018, 7; Sabourin 1997, 11).

From Personal to Political: Moral Landscapes of a Multi-Situated Researcher

Conducting feminist research,[4] I do not consider production of knowledge as neutral, but rather as a mediated process that can (re)produce gender norms, and representations, resulting in bias contrary to the claim of 'objectivity' (Martin 1991; Reinharz 1992). Therefore, I follow Harding's invitation to reveal the political motives behind my research on a quest for 'strong objectivity', in order to clarify the social location and historicity of the situated knowledge I have produced (Delphy 2009; Harding 1987, 438). My epistemological point of departure is not one of 'break' but of standpoint theory (Bourdieu *et al.* 1983, 27; Wylie

---

[3] 'Jeune fille' is the expression used to express this status. It is borrowed from French and opposed to 'Madame', which refers to a married woman.

[4] If feminist research can be described as 'primarily connected to feminist struggle', in the sense that it aims to challenge 'the basic structures and ideologies that oppress women' by 'illuminating gender-based stereotypes and biases, and unearthing women's subjugated knowledge', it draws from a wide range of methodologies (Brooks and Nagy Hesse-Biber 2014, 4).

2003, 26). Reflecting on my own embodiment of gender relations is thus important for understanding how I *personally* perceive and experience them, and how this, in turn, affects and is reflected in the terms and the way in which I *professionally* delimitate the object of my study (De Gasquet 2015). Moreover, the choice of an ethnographic approach involves my presence and participation in social relations during the fieldwork, which in turn requires an analysis of its effects on knowledge production (Campigotto *et al.* 2017; Munthali 2001; Ouattara 2004).

Feminist anthropologists offer a rich analysis of the ways in which their work is shaped by the different facets of one's social position, particularly with regards to their choice of subject, the method of data collection, and its interpretation. In *Arab Women in the Field: Studying Your Own Society* (Altorki and Fawzi El-Solh 1988), I found a valuable framework for reflecting upon the impact the status of 'indigenous woman' has on the social experience of female researchers in societies in which sexual segregation, to different extents, continues to structure the social reality. Relying on their narratives, I will unpack the personal and activist reasons motivating the choice to conduct research on Algerian society, and the feminist motive behind working on topics at the crossroads of gender and Islam. As I recognise that my research is a professional path, shaped by my intersecting identities, and part of a broader personal journey, unveiling some of my intimate details here is necessary in order to contextualise the subsequent analysis of the ethical choices I made during fieldwork.

A Personal and Political Quest for Recovering Memory

One of the experiences that decidedly motivate my research is situated in the uprooting that occurred during my late childhood as I left the African continent as an eleven-year-old, in the context of an armed conflict. Upon my arrival in Switzerland, I found myself thrown into a completely different society, and an entirely different social position.[5] Indeed, the process of transplantation led to a first splitting in two of my Self, forcing out my Algerian 'double', and fading away its memories. A European double, shaped in a liberal environment, was under construction. Burying the traces of my childhood deep down

5   Described by Jacquet (2014) as 'transclass', a term that refers to a process of 'non-social reproduction', under exceptional political, social, economic, and familial circumstances, resulting in the passage from one social class to another, and affecting the constitution of individuals.

without dealing with the trauma of the war would span several years (Akello 2012, 290). Eventually, I reached a turning point where the social distance – amplified by the effect of time – had transformed the geographical distance into a cultural trench between myself and my relatives and childhood friends.

As my European double had internalised, during those years, it now embodied a figure of ethnical 'Otherness'. Thus, my inner desire to return home could be framed as an organic need to reconnect that part of myself to its original mirror.[6] This explains why I began my research in Algeria since I perceive myself as a native. My own relatives, however, would see me as a reflection of the Other by referring to me as an immigrant.

In fact, from the outset, my status placed me as a mid-sider, holding characteristics of both 'here' (through features of ethnicity such as the place of birth, filiation, use of Algerian dialect, religious knowledge, and so on) and 'there' (through features of social class such as self-presentation, use of foreign languages, nationality, currency, and so on). Witnessing the alteration of the time that passed, I was struck both by how my seat in my relatives' domestic spaces was always guaranteed, as if the years did not alter the familial tie, and by how my presence as a mid-sider seemed to trouble my family, as if I was blurring the line,[7] demarcating the 'in' from the 'out', and thus threatening familial self-preservation.

Once again, I tasted snippets of the happy memories of my childhood, rediscovered the atmosphere of domestic spaces, the rhythms of domestic tasks, the daily social life (coffee with the neighbours, Ramadan evenings amongst friends), and all sorts of celebrations for special occasions (weddings, circumcisions, or births). The more time I spent in these spaces and the more I roamed the streets, woke up, went to sleep, talked, ate, bathed, the more the memories

---

[6] Before starting this research at the age of 28, I had undertaken other projects in Arabic speaking countries, where I was partly seeking to rediscover my primary cultural environment. The hazards of research in volatile political contexts are what drove me to working in Algeria for such a long time, and to participate intensely again in my family and community, by returning to the suburbs of Algiers.

[7] As in the words of Joseph, it is not only the fact of living abroad that is at stake here, but of living in the 'West' (as the Lebanese expression in her case points clearly: 'mughtaribi'), that constitutes the source of alteration by living surrounded by/at the 'Others' (cited in Altorki and Fawzi El-Solh 1988, 1088).

of my body resurfaced in my consciousness. Little by little, my body found its bearings as it felt immersed in this familiar environment. As of that point, these two life forms began to coexist in a way so complex that it seemed paradoxical; by experiencing circumstances in which I did not understand the issues of social representation, I was gaining awareness of my own social amnesia caused by my prolonged absence. I constantly felt out of sync. The more I became re-indigenised, the more I became aware of my European double, whereas I had previously laboured under the illusion of having a single, unified Me (Kondo 1986). As a kind of revenant who was witnessing the spectacle of her own duplication, I experienced the 'ghostly paradigm' to which Mbembe (2013, 215) refers, in which there is neither reversibility nor irreversibility of time, and 'only the winding of experiences matters'.

During these two years spent in the field, throughout which I moved between Algeria and Europe, I often felt myself drifting, torn between my different identities. I experienced considerable emotional turbulence (often feeling lost in translation) (Rémy 2014). The more I immersed myself into Algerian society – discerning, remembering, and feeling once more – the more I realised how difficult it was to be back again in Europe for short stays. In the long run, the slow reconnection with the shadow of the little girl buried within me, who lived amongst her own people and projected herself as an indigenous person in the narrative of her ancestors, helped in balancing out the space taken up by her European double (that had internalised the embodying of a representation of an outsider in a European context). In brief, fieldwork, to me, did not only consist of a movement through space, but also through time by rediscovering the land of my ancestors in order to reconnect with the community of my own (Bodson 2000).

Personally, finding my way back home helped to heal the traumas that the political violence of my childhood had left, as if recovering memory undid the social division and hostility that had kept me away so long, and helped reinterpret them in an appeased and comprehensive effort to produce a memory of the experience (see Sabourin 1997). Therefore, I hope that writing as an outsider-within in the academy contributes to the ongoing establishment of a memory of the traces left by a decade of political violence, and to consider how its ghosts still shape everyday life despite the population's attempt to resilience (Hill Collins 1986, 14). Such objectives are hampered by the political amnesia imposed at the beginning of the millennium, but living in the diaspora and holding an emergency exit card (my passport) constituted a privilege, and from my point of view a responsibility, from which my family and I can benefit (Moussaoui 2006).

An Activist Call to Decolonising Feminism

Beyond holding an Algerian identity, I grew up as a little girl during the 1980s and 1990s in the suburbs of Algiers, in a society that sought to maintain the spatial segregation of gender relations, despite the growing difficulty of faithfully reproducing a traditional patriarchal 'arrangement between the sexes' in an urban setting (Goffman and Zaidman 2003; Mace 2015). Throughout my childhood, I was largely immersed in the domestic, and predominantly feminine, sphere. These gatherings of sisters, cousins, and friends were moments of solidarity in which women shared the joys and troubles of their domestic lives, caring about each other and emotionally 'merging' together (Joseph 1988, 39). As they helped, advised, and listened to one another, I was struck by how their common experience of vulnerability as women in a male-dominated system was the foundation of their solidarity, despite their socio-economic or cultural disparities.

At the same time, I was scarred by the power relations linked to gender and by the violence I witnessed around me, and to which I was being groomed by society. My awareness of the injustice against the category of female was heightened by the stark contrast between the education I was receiving within my family and the norms which applied outside my home. Access to education for girls was, admittedly, a political right, but it did not seem to hold the same importance as it did for boys in the eyes of some families and teachers that legitimised discriminatory practices by referring to a religious authority. Hence, school soon became a space in which I would acquire my autonomy and my thirst for recognition as an individual.

From a very young age, my personal experience of being assigned a subordinate role as a female, together with the fact that I witnessed these networks of solidarity, instilled in me a spirit of resistance, which turned into a feminist consciousness. This feminist consciousness never ceased growing over time. As an adult, this feminist awakening led me to seek ways in which to act upon it beyond my personal sphere. Discovering the critical dimension of the social sciences, and particularly that of feminist epistemology, my research focused upon Islamic feminism. It is a movement that delegitimises the subordination of women to a male guardianship through the reinterpretation of Islamic religious doctrine. Learning more about the experiences of these women in a European context made me want to understand the obstacles to forging alliances between secular and Islamic feminists in Belgium (Djelloul 2018a). I was particularly struck by the denial of the latter's feminist consciousness, because rooting their speech in Islam would be a contradiction in terms. When presenting the results in either secular feminist or Muslim environments, I often felt like these women could not be recognised either as feminist, nor as Muslim because they were assigned to dichotomic categories, which did not allow a bridge for a common horizon to appear (Mbembe 2013). In this context, I was inspired by Mestiri's (2016) recent suggestion to decolonise feminism by adopting a transcultural approach that navigates along its border, allowing a plurality of feminisms to emerge.

When I arrived in Algeria in 2014, I wanted to carry on understanding how religion could be used as a tool to challenge women's oppression, focusing my attention on a nascent dynamic of feminisation of the religious field. Still at an exploratory stage, I was planning to visit the Islamic faculties of several universities in the country to have the chance to meet female students. However, nothing turned out as expected. I underestimated how returning home would be difficult to handle. I would be travelling through different sets of gender norms, which would impose constraints and a new perspective to my research. I had to learn how to cover up as a female and to cover up my family's secrets before being able to conduct research.

From a Constraint to a Resource: The Disguise of Dutiful Daughter as a Cover for a Researcher Trapped in a Domestic Moral Economy

I landed in Algiers a few weeks after my mother had returned from Europe after seventeen years of absence. I had planned to spend a few days with her and my relatives before breaking ground on my research by wandering through the city. But I immediately faced several attempts to discourage me from leaving the inside. I was pointed to the physical abuse and the moral damage my presence outside would provoke, to me and my family. I started wondering about my lack of awareness of the current security situation in Algeria and whether I would be able to conduct my research. My family's subsequent outcry at any of my attempts to go out proved to be so severe, and their insistence on accompanying me so unavoidable, that I started questioning the notion they were assuming of my evident vulnerability as a woman.

Experiencing spatial containment was hard psychologically as I felt imprisoned, surrounded by domestic walls and emotionally exposed all the time, constantly on daughter duty under the watch and control of my extended family (Foucault 1975). No visit could be declined, no question avoided, and once guests were there, I could not leave the scene without losing face, both for me and my parents. I quickly realised how unprepared I was to face these family politics because of my long absence and the distance it had created with my relatives. Fortunately, other social characteristics allowed me to gain some flexibility with regard to gender roles. First, as an immigrant, I represented both an 'outsider' who had been altered by another cultural context, and a 'transclass', who now held sufficient economic resources to access autonomous and safe transportation from the suburbs to downtown and other cities. This status granted me some leeway with my behaviour because it partially shielded my relatives from the shame that my behaviour could incite and relieved them of responsibility when I would challenge the patriarchal norm.[8]

The first weeks of confinement and of trying out strategies to get more spatial mobility sparked my interest in how other women managed to go out despite this 'familial containment' and how they experienced the extra-domestic spaces (Djelloul 2018b). Therefore, I decided to turn the constraint of staying 'inside' to my advantage and to start observing while I participated (I had to) in domestic spaces. Starting my ethnography from my parents' and relatives' homes turned out to be very useful, even though it definitely blurred the divide between on- and off-duty during the fieldwork experience, leading to specific ethical dilemmas which I recount below.

On the one hand, it gave me the necessary data to better understand the specifics of my position in the lineage (as a non-married woman). It also helped me to grasp the social location of the discourses and the practices (on family, marriage, and religion) I witnessed or participated in, in the broader Algerian social landscape (class, gender, and ethnicity). This background information was crucial to contextualising and clarifying my parents' trajectories from my own. Actively engaging in the social relations at home also helped me catch up on

---

8   In other words, I excused them from having to publicly admit that they had failed to pass on and enforce this norm. On the contrary, when I did behave myself in a manner deemed 'decent for an immigrant', my behaviour even brought them pride as though this was proof that they had indeed carried out their mission.

the missed time and update my skills as a dutiful daughter (cooking, presenting, and serving the food, performing a gendered self-presentation through attributes of femininity such as straight hair, make up, and so on). Once I had developed enough skills and networks to leave domestic spaces covered to meet women outside my familial circles, the amount of time I had spent with my relatives proved to be a serious advantage to getting access to interviewees. By that time, I had the right(eous) behaviours and proper attitudes allowing me to visit them at home without hurting their families with my previous shameless reactions. By agreeing to play by the dutiful daughter's rules,[9] I was credited with the moral capital needed to enter and stay in other people's homes; I was covered by my family's social standing and reputation.

On the other hand, being trapped by a social group in the field proved to be a challenging source of ethical dilemmas. I faced contradictory loyalties; between my responsibility towards my relatives whose moral capital I maintained by covering up sources of 'shame' and my commitment towards the scientific community not to deceive interviewees, in order to build relationships based on mutual trust.

Protected and Governed by the Costume of a Dutiful Daughter

My return home without a remarkable change of position (as non-married) immediately returned me to the status of dutiful daughter, with its rights and responsibilities. This situation provided some advantages. The first was the legitimacy of my presence there, since as my parents' dutiful daughter, I neither needed to negotiate my entry, nor the conditions and length of my stay in the field.

---

9   I left Algeria as a child (before puberty when women generally start experiencing spatial confinement), and because when I went back I was always accompanied by my parents, I had not realised how much women's spatial mobility, in other words the social capacity they are given to move beyond family's domestic spaces, was anything but self-evident, and rather a matter of power relations within the family. Deciding to find a place on my own would have been very difficult (as it is rare for a landlord to rent to non-married women), dangerous since I would be considered deviant living outside familial guardianship, and costly because such a choice would have caused my banishment and that of my parents (held responsible for my behaviours) from many of my relatives.

Second, my pre-existing cultural background was priceless in helping me understand the normative issues at stake or, at least, the reactions that suggested when something in the social interactions went wrong, even if I did not understand why immediately. The third advantage was a gendered habitus that, as Joseph (1988, 39) describes, has predisposed me to 'merge' emotionally in my social relations, 'by feeling "little sense of my boundaries" and seeming to dive into relationships with people'". Therefore, I had no problem adapting to Algerian traditional familial codes when visiting family.

However, I underestimated the extent to which my role as a dutiful daughter would also limit my social capacity to act and would position me as socially subordinate. As mentioned previously, living abroad, I was not reproducing that model. I thought that I had long since overcome the guilt that had shrouded me in these family ties. Therefore, it was very challenging to expose myself, once again, to these power relations. Indeed, as someone who was raised as a dutiful daughter, I had internalised 'the standards of female modesty', along with the power relations that structure a family unit (Abu Lughod 1988, 141; Joseph 1988, 36). Hence, my obvious recalcitrance over recognising the authority of my elders and my male relatives created tensions at the outset of my work. My reservations towards merging in relationships with other women could be challenging as their expectations infringed on my sense of personhood and Self. My ways of resisting by asserting my individual freedom portrayed me as a shameless girl (the opposite of a dutiful daughter), who would reject the norms the familial group had transmitted to her as a child.

My behaviour was particularly harmful to my mother, who was materially sheltering me and morally covering for me as a non-married woman. At the beginning, I did not understand how my behaviour hurt her reputation, as she was seen as responsible for my lack of shame. She begged me to foresee the consequences of what I would say and do because '[it] would reflect on my image and that of my family', starting with her own (Abu Lughod, 1988, 154). My mother often warned me how much, as a single female, my respectability and reputation were of crucial concern since no man, except my father who lived abroad, was there to act as a guardian and protect me from outsiders.

In addition to raising my awareness, my mother also played a crucial part in the smooth progress of my fieldwork. She mediated between the other family members and myself, served as a kind of bridge while making up for my blunders. She also sometimes accompanied me to other people's homes when I was meeting other women who experienced the same familial containment. My mother's presence was essential to removing a barrier of protection between myself and my interviewees' relatives. It proved that as much as I was an immigrant, I had not yet reached a level of insubordination that would lead me to scorn the family norms, such as being morally uncovered (namely moving outside the home without a guardian). My mother thus embodied a moral bridge between me and some interviewees by covering up the potential threat I embodied, as a mid-sider, to their families' reputation.

As well as belonging to an honourable family, my Arabic linguistic abilities were highly useful in lessening the cultural distance created between myself, and my status as an immigrant, and my interlocutors. It highlighted my interest in my national identity, which included both Arabness and Islam (Carlier 1995). Both were automatically assumed to derive from my status as a dutiful daughter. My occasional participation in certain religious rites, such as praying at the mosque, was the source of congratulations and encouragement. I was perceived as being on the right track to my way back home.

On the one hand, sharing other women's constraints to spatial mobility constitutes very rich material that helps me understand and further question the spatial mobility in an intersectional way through gender, class, and ethnic lenses (Bilge 2009; Le Renard 2010, 129). On the other hand, being trapped spatially as a researcher forced me to navigate through different layers of family politics and intense ethical dilemmas. Having part of my identity from here, I am entitled to respect the moral codes of honourable families and to internalise that my behaviours as a woman-researcher are a matter of public concern, tying me to my family.

Protecting Familial Ties by Telling Pious Lies

Shamy and Altorki, in their respective contributions to *Arab Women in the Field* (1988), explain that while the difficulty for an anthropologist perceived as an 'outsider' is to gain a group's trust, the difficulty for an 'insider' is found in the threat that she poses to the group, with whom she shares its dirty laundry and secrets. Indeed, after the first period of initiation during which I could not distinguish trivial information from secrets that should be kept locked inside the familial ties, I progressively learnt how to cover up information from the outsiders, by staying silent, pretending to ignore the rumours, not panicking, and not conceding facts when I heard them. Developing this social covering-up skill demanded a lot of time to understand the normative issues and power relations at stake, in addition to self-control, emotional opacity, and a sense of moral commitment towards the group.

Yet another ethical challenge I met in order to maintain a dutiful daughter's face was to deal with the fact that my honest answers to several questions immediately asked by distant relatives or outsiders would not only cause displeasure, but also risked damaging my parents' reputation, or even my entire extended family if the word got around. These were questions related to my personal life or my brothers' and sisters' – who lived abroad – way of life (i.e. moral conduct) and could be part of strategies to undermine my family's reputation. The general ethical standard of not deceiving your interviewees prevented me from lying to the subjects of my study, and I felt trapped as the survival of my social face, and that of my familial group, demanded that I conceal what would be a source of shame.

As a last resort, I produced what some would call a pious lie, meaning a lie for the family's sake. As familial ties are considered sacred, it is supposed to be morally acceptable to lie in order to prevent harm, or shock, or provoking the envy of a family member, or bringing shame to the family in the judgment of an outsider. Although I was, for a long time, uncomfortable with these kinds of little arrangements with morality, I had to overcome my requirements for honesty. I became aware that the need to maintain my family's honour was greater than my personal moral qualms. My duty as a family member, benefiting from its cover in front of the others, forced me to put my moral choice into an ethical perspective. In the Algerian context, ethics do not derive from an individualistic moral choice – as in a liberal environment – but constitutes a public matter and a moral economy that helps to reproduce families and communities by protecting them from the threat of individual desires.

I have chosen not to discuss the pious lies I had to invent or reproduce for the sake of my parents' social reputation, but I want to stress that, despite the moral principle of honesty and the ethical commitment to building relations based on trust, lying for self-preservation was essential in that context to prevent harming my relatives, and de facto, myself, as a person, and a researcher.

Interference as a Source of Trouble, and the Outsider's Reflection in my Eyes

When research and personal lives merge, it creates an intense experience, where 'an autoethnographic self-narration may be risky to self-identity' because it troubles the perception of the Self (Butz and Besio 2009, 1661). Since fieldwork cannot be fully anticipated, deontological issues sometimes only appear afterwards. Doing research 'at home' has led me to view ethics as an ongoing process, and not as fixed norms, evolving with me throughout the field. The critical move of reflexivity is made possible by the intersubjective setting of writing. Those new lenses on the memory *in* the experience, informed by the experience itself, help them to produce a 'memory *of* the experience' (Halbwachs 1997, 18, emphasis added).

As I reach the final stage of writing up my findings, I realise that unrevealed ethical choices extend until this point: how far can I anonymise a relative, such as my own mother? How can I remain transparent to my reader while pursuing academic objectivity if it demands that I reveal the secrets of my relatives? This leads us to the necessary ethical quagmire that arises from choosing to start my ethnography at home; the impossibility of keeping a social distance with my participants while being immersed in the field (see also Vuninga in this book).

Critical reflexivity has helped me acknowledge, after my fieldwork, how my relatives had been affected by my conduct in the field, because my objectifying eye somehow violated their 'intimacy' in domestic spaces. Even though I understand my behaviours as a response to a great vulnerability experienced in the field, I will now consider how to minimise the damages my presence has caused. At this stage of writing, I have chosen to dismiss some data, or veil the familial ties in order to ensure continuous consent and protection of anonymity, even though I could not promise that I would do no harm. Finally, I try to find my own voice's way through my relatives' expectations, without betraying them.

Disrupting the Scene by Interfering on the Familial Stage

After a few weeks spent in Algeria, my project was becoming more concrete, and I began to clearly spell out the professional motive behind my presence, and my interest in the mobility of women. The questions I asked were henceforth perceived as forming part of a study, even though they were not asked in the context of a formal interview. And yet, my relatives were happy to be able to help me, and to share their opinions and assessments of Algerian society.

Family visits allowed me, as a witness to these meetings, to be kept up-to-date about the news in each family. I witnessed and listened to every one of their conversations, as I had in my earliest childhood, but without ever explicitly being the addressee of their words. Yet, I was less interested in the facts they were reporting than in the interpretations these implied, which revealed the norms that were at stake. I therefore started asking questions, interfering in their conversations, seeking clarifications about the stories to which they referred, and asked them to explain their opinions on a certain person or what they were implying. While I thought my questions were harmless enough, I sometimes intruded – without knowing – upon secrets shared by some relatives, and which they did not want to divulge.

Sometimes their silence was enough for me to understand I had gone too far. Other times, I only realised after the fact that I might have hurt some people present, because I insisted on getting an explanation that would implicate, indirectly, a third person present (or one of their relatives). Because these family reunions are also a stage for competition between lineages, in which everybody performs a play, I sometimes broke the *illusio* of the scene through my interrogations, trying to understand what was at stake. For an insider, the answers should have been socially self-evident.

My immodest behaviours (such as springing questions on my hosts, and giving direct opinions) were a reminder of the potential threat I represented for the familial unit (as are other outsiders).

Time only made me realise how much I could have been considered as a threat to my own relatives, especially due to the fact that I was an immigrant, and I didn't know how to play family politics well enough. Only after several months in the field, had I internalised a specific, embodied sensibility of my social status in Algeria, through which I sought to maintain my rank as a 'dutiful daughter' (while negotiating the expectations and gender codes as an immigrant woman). Even if considered a mid-sider, I was more at ease in participating in family gatherings and following the proper behaviour without harming anyone. I had learnt how to ask questions in a roundabout manner, to know when I should hold my tongue, and how to read between the lines to understand what my interlocutor was implying.

Afterwards, I could only express regret for these deontological missteps (intrusion, harm, pious lies). However, the last ethical choice I made was not to use the information collected as data. Moreover, the impossibility of guaranteeing total anonymity to my relatives led me to partially cover up the preliminary phase of my research in my family's domestic spaces by moving away from a narrative autoethnography that emphasises 'the ethnographic dialogue or encounter' (Butz and Besio 2009, 1666). Through an ethnography from 'below' (or subaltern), I rather focus on the movement it produced between my doubles, by stressing that 'autoethnography is itself a source and outcome of transcultural identity formation' (Butz and Besio 2009, 1668).

The Threatening Colonial Ghost of my European Double

Throughout my fieldwork, through my family's mediation, I felt a growing sense of loyalty and guilt toward them. I was nagged by the question of what I could reveal about them without being indecent, namely without betraying them. As my relationships with them strengthened, I felt a responsibility to protect them from what would be said about them over there (by the outsiders) and realised how much my corporeality as an immigrant could have been perceived as an intrusion from the outside. This ambiguous status stressed that, despite my formal quality as a member of the group, my stay elsewhere had somehow irreversibly altered me. I thus represented a kind of mirror for my interlocutors; in facing me, they sought to either conform or demarcate themselves from a model they perceived as 'Other' (or Western, meaning non-Muslim, non-believer, shameless, immoral) through their discourses and practices.

Beyond my familial circles, my recovery of home increased my sense of belonging to the land of my ancestors. The process of re-indigenisation, through which I recognised and distanced myself from my European double, made me more aware of how its colonial ghost was perceived as threatening my people's self-representation and narratives. My interlocutors would both be suspicious about what my European double would think, as they explained the virtues of Algerian society to me (the beauty of the traditional flavours of Ramadan, the importance of visiting sick people in Muslim society), as if they anticipated a negative opinion from me on these traditions and beliefs. At the same time, they also felt a certain pride that I would still care about my society of origin, that I would hold on to my blood. Settling down again after having travelled abroad seemed to prove that this 'land' was worth the try, that my Algerian identity was still a source of pride. Were they trying to compensate for a loss of face in front of a 'symbolic domination' (Landry 2006, 85)?

It seems to me, looking at it from here and now, that an intersubjective setting was taking place through my presence: everything leads me to think I embodied an external and judgmental eye, to whom people wanted to prove that their religion – as the cornerstone of their collective/national identity – was dignified. Beyond me personally, I believe people were seeking out the colonial ghost of my European double, trying to lay it to rest. Progressively, through mediation and time, I started to be expected to represent and be the spokesperson of my people, namely Algerian, African, Muslims, Arabs, and so on.

As a researcher, I refuse to represent any of those categories that would cause me to avoid self-criticism. But beyond self-censorship, I am serious about taking on the responsibility not to misrepresent contemporary Algerian society. Hence, as I think and write about Africa from its diaspora, I feel committed about dismantling an interpretation framework that would fill a 'fantasy well' by reproducing an orientalist image of 'otherness' (Mbembe 2013, 65). To me, writing against culture as Abu Lughod (1996) suggests, means writing against a colonial ghost that haunts the mirror of the Selves, of both the subject and object of research.

Multi-Situated Ethics as a Continuous Process of Critical Reflexivity

Ethical dilemmas interrupt throughout the road of research; even if the moral landscape of the researcher is made explicit to identify the social location of the person, social mediations cannot all be anticipated, nor can their effect on the knowledge that will be produced. Autoethnography is a tool that can turn into a dangerous mirror for the Self, especially when it threatens to expose intimate familial ties. Therefore, the role of critical reflexivity is to limit the effects of exposing reflexivity of the Self, in order to protect from or repair ethical violations on the participants from the objectifying eyes of the researcher, who is on a quest for strong objectivity.

I take responsibility for my voice as a mid-sider, one that tries to describe the frontiers experienced at the crossroads of gender, class, and ethnicity. Throughout my movement between different spaces, times, and languages, as I recovered my memory, I understood the 'ghosts' that inhabit my various doubles as self-representations of social reality. Since I want to contribute to decolonial feminist research, admitting my own multiplicity is important because it allows me to acknowledge the different standpoints I embody, and make explicit the movement between them. Multi-situating my writing forces me to be socially located as a mid-sider, who adapts to different audiences (and their specific political debates), without reproducing the borders between those social locations. Instead, I aim to build bridges to contribute to the intersubjective transcultural space, in which I, as a Self, can move between my doubles, in a 'travelling identity' (Mbembe 2013, 145).

Further Reading

Butz, David, and Kathryn Besio. 2009. 'Autoethnography'. *Geography Compass* 3, no. 5: 1660–74.

Kondo, Dorinne. 1986. 'Dissolution and Reconstitution of Self: Implications for Anthropological Epistemology'. *Cultural Anthropology* 1, no. 1: 74–88.

Mestiri, Soumaya. 2016. *Décoloniser le féminisme: une approche transculturelle*. Paris: Vrin.

Pratt, Mary Louise. 1994. 'Transculturation and Autoethnography: Peru, 1615/1980'. In *Colonial Discourse/Postcolonial Theory*, edited by Francis Barker, Peter Hulme, and Margaret Iverson, 24–46. Manchester: Manchester University Press.

4

Establishing Kinship in the Diaspora: Conducting Research among Fellow Congolese Immigrants of Cape Town

Rosette Sifa Vuninga

M Y EXPERIENCE AS an 'insider', researching fellow Congolese immigrants of Cape Town, South Africa, has been shaped by a number of challenges in the 'field'. Over time, I noticed a growing rift between my research participants and myself. Two major factors explain this. The first is what most participants perceived as my advanced level of education, as a doctoral candidate in history. The second is the increasing politicisation of ethno-regional feuds among Congolese transnational communities in Cape Town (Garbin and Godin 2013; Inaka 2016). Thus, my Congolese participants neither accepted me as an insider nor as an outsider. My personal and professional identities merged, as I morphed from being just a fellow Congolese immigrant from the Kivu region to an intellectual woman pursuing her doctoral degree in South Africa.

In this chapter, I discuss the challenges of fieldwork among the Congolese of Cape Town. The first is around the methodological challenges of being an ethnographic 'inbetweener' despite my sense of being an 'insider' (Milligan 2016). As Unluer (2012, 2) explains, 'insider-research-ers are those who choose to study a group to which they belong'. I con-sidered myself an insider among the Congolese refugee communities of Cape Town because since my arrival in 2004, I too have experienced the financial hardships and xenophobia of South Africa (Neocosmos 2010; Owen 2015; Pugh 2014).

The second challenge relates to the broader issues of ethical practice in ethnographic fieldwork, the one Tolich (2004, 102) describes as having 'the potential to harm both researchers and their informants'. By 'harm', I am referring to my persistence in accessing the research field even when there were signs and feelings of mistrust and avoidance, not just from my research participants, but also from me to them. This is because in some instances, I felt discomfort in their willingness to par-ticipate in my research in the sense that their participation could clash with the golden ethical rule of 'do no harm' (Mackenzie *et al.* 2007; Thomson 2013b). Thus, like other researchers who have found them-selves in a similar position, I often complied to 'make active attempts to place' myself 'in between' an insider and outsider in my research field-work, a position I sometimes felt was unfairly imposed on me (Milligan 2016, 248). How this happened and how I managed my 'inbetweener' status is discussed in this chapter. Although the focus of this chapter is on my doctorate research fieldwork (2016–2017), I provide a brief back-ground from when I started researching among the Congolese in Cape Town mainly to demonstrate the changes both in my research position-ing (by myself and my participants) and changes in issues related to both my methodology and my ethical sensibilities.

The complexity of navigating everyday life in Cape Town, as Con-golese immigrants must, motivated me to adopt an ethnographic approach. I was also confident in my knowledge of my research site and 'subjects' from my past experience (for my honours and master's programme), from being one of them (as a Congolese immigrant who has lived in South Africa for over a decade), and from possessing the necessary language skills, including fluency in Kiswahili, Lingala, and French. But mostly, I understood ethnography as 'a unique method for investigating the enormously rich, complex, conflictual, problematic, and diverse experiences, thoughts, feelings, and activities of human beings and the meanings of their existence' (Jorgensen 1989, 1). My chapter considers the ethical challenges and opportunities of being an inbetweener that are also inherent in the ethnographic method, that were in turn, largely shaped by the dynamics of home country and host country (see also Djelloul in this volume on being a 'mid-sider').

A Congolese researcher of Congolese

When I arrived in Cape Town in June 2004, I held refugee status until I received my Permanent Resident's identification document in early 2016. And, before I received a full academic scholarship to pursue doctoral studies in 2015, I was just an ordinary Congolese refugee woman. I had juggled being a full-time waitress and bartender and being a full-time student at the University of the Western Cape (UWC) since 2008, when I enrolled in the undergraduate programme. It was not until 2012 that I earned a renewable tutorial contract at UWC's History department. While living on a study wage was (and remains) not entirely satisfactory for me, I have, for many of my Congolese compatriots, achieved remarkable socio-economic mobility. This, I must admit, is not an everyday reality for refugees in South Africa. However, as a woman living 'alone' and from a relatively modest family, there are various interpretations of my success among my fellow countrymen. For some, being an unmarried woman could mean I have 'secret helpers' who make it possible for me to afford a university education and other basic needs. Others associate my success with my ethnic and regional identity, in particular those from Kinshasa who are not shy to ask me if I am a beneficiary of those scholarships that certain refugee organisations give only to people from the Kivu region. There is validity in their perception as scarce South African resources are available for Congolese refugees who fled the DRC's warzones, in the east of the country where I grew up. This is mostly because since the mid-2000s, South African migration policies make clear distinctions between Congolese refugees (Kivucians in general) and economic migrants (mostly Congolese from Kinshasa and other perceived peaceful regions of the DRC).

Worth mentioning too, is the fact that my research is conducted during the era of emergent Congolese transnational political activities that are shaped by 'ethnicity, regionalism, and political rivalries' which informed the post-2011 elections crisis in the DRC and transnationally in the Congolese diaspora (Inaka 2016, 5. See also Garbin and Godin 2013; Godin and Dona 2016). This led to tensions between Congolese from the eastern and western regions of the country, in the form of the rise of a Combattants movement – a 'pressure group' claiming most of the radical activism among Congolese transnationals in Western countries as well as in South Africa (Vuninga 2017). This ethno-regionalism regularly preceded me in the field. In fact, since the 2011 elections, one's region of origin or ethnic identity can stereotypically be used to assume one's political allegiance (mostly in relation to being pro-Kabilist or anti-Kabilist). This state of affairs largely shaped the ways in which my identity as a woman researcher from Kivu impacted on my research fieldwork including the ways in which some participants raised their concerns regarding my research topic, my methodology, as well as the motivations of my research and whose ends it served. Because of this, my fieldwork was challenged by various ethical dilemmas that I had not encountered in my previous research fieldworks. Suspicions character-ised most of my interview interactions, a far cry from my presumption of open, frank, and trust-based relationships with my participants. They would soon consider me an inbetweener long before I even knew they considered me as such.

Fieldwork Then and Now

In 2011, I began ethnographic research among the Congolese of Cape Town as part of my honours programme. I was excited about doing it for the first time after lectures on how ethnography has been a crucial tool in the work of social historians (Bank and Bank 2013; Bozzoli 1985; Vansina 1985). I felt that an ethnographic approach, which includes the use of semi-structured interviews, focus group discussions, and observation used by social historians, was best suited to study how Congolese women understood and experienced xenophobia in Cape Town (Bozzoli 1985; Bozzoli and Nkotsoe 1993). My research participants were also more welcoming and willing to provide any information I needed from them. To a large extent, my participants were comfortable with xenophobia as a topic of conver-sation. Many had lived through the infamous April and May 2008 xenophobic attacks in South Africa, an event that made both local and international headlines (Neocosmos 2010).

To a large extent, I was received as, and indeed considered myself an 'insider'. I was researching 'my "own" people', with whom I shared a variety of identities including 'background, culture and faith' as well as being a refugee woman from the DRC resident in Cape Town (Gregory and Ruby 2011, 168; Merriam *et al.* 2001). My participants included close friends who introduced me to their other female friends, relatives, and associates of all sorts. Others were my work colleagues at the restaurant where I worked at the time and other places I have worked before. I also interacted with my hairdresser, who introduced me to other Congolese women hairdressers. Others I first met in the long queues at Home Affairs during applications and renewal of my refugee papers. I interviewed female partners and wives. These women (and some men) were highly supportive of my education because a good number of them held the *graduat* (a three-year university degree in the DRC) or *licence* (a five-year university degree, and approximate to the South African honours degree that I was pursuing at the time). We communicated about meetings using cell phone calls and text messages. I saw the close relationship I had with the main participants as an ethical opportunity given the availability and excitement of most of them in wanting to participate in my research.

I must admit that being unaware of the challenges of doing research as an insider contributed to the confidence and optimism with which I conducted my honours mini-thesis fieldwork. Indeed, it did not even cross my mind that I was an insider, let alone the limits of researching among friends (Brewis 2014). For example, Brewis (2014, 856) warns against the ethical dangers of 'ex-ante' data, which is using information one knew about the friends-participants prior to being a researcher among them. In my case, I often used much of this information from my previous talks about my friends not being aware of the potential ethical implications. All I knew is that if I used information that was not given to me with consent for research participation, I had to keep the source anonymous. At least that is what we were told once in one of our workshops on quoting voices in our honours-level writing. How I selected my participants, however, was simply by interviewing those people who were the most open, available, and willing. Both the emotional connection that I felt with them, and the intimate conversations that they openly shared, were used in selecting my main research participants.

All the same, I was not confined to ethical research protocols by my institution for conducting ethnographic research for my honours mini-thesis, as later became the case for my MA and PhD programmes. I knew that researchers experience difficulties in ethnographic research since we discussed them in some workshops on 'oral history' and research on everyday life, which rely mostly on life histories (Bozzoli and Nkotsoe 1991; Gluck and Patai 2016). However, I was certain that I would not face difficulties in accessing potential interviewees because I was using my friends and their friends as my participants. Therefore, I could not care less about 'ethical challenges and emotional pitfalls' that could haunt me while conducting ethnography among my own people (Thomson *et al.* 2013, 1). I even engaged in Congolese habits of 'home' as useful tools of my fieldwork, such as just showing up at someone's house or workspace without an appointment. Other individuals, including hairdressers, shopkeepers, security guards, and street vendors I knew, welcomed me to their workplaces and businesses anytime I showed up, with or without an appointment.

These informal meetings were reciprocal; I felt there was no power imbalance between my participants and me. For example, we met at my place a few times for focus group discussions where we would share a soda, biscuits, or a home cooked meal I prepared for the meeting. But generally, they preferred that I go to them. Time, transport costs, and all the stresses related to travelling to my residence were among the reasons why participants preferred that I travel to meet them. I also visited others at their houses and the amount of hospitality I received was more family- and friendship-related while in the meantime, they became so used to the idea that during those days all our meetings were about my studies. Hence, they would serve me a drink or something to eat then, almost automatically ask, 'So, what do you want us to talk about today?' or 'About what we were talking about last time, I forgot to mention that...' And we would immediately begin the discussion in Kiswahili, or Lingala, or French, mixing with some English. Sometimes, each of these languages were used in an interview with one person.

The best way to describe my position in the field during my honours programme is by using Taylor's (2011) concept of 'intimate insider' which embeds the positive effects of researching among 'friend-in-formants' in contrast with 'informant-friends':

> 'Intimate insider research' can be distinguished from 'insider research' on the basis that the researcher is working, at the deepest level, within their own 'backyard'; that is, a contemporary cultural space with which the researcher has regular and ongoing contact; where the researcher's personal relationships are deeply embedded in the field; where one's quotidian interactions and performances of identity are made visible; where the researcher has been and remains a key social actor within the field and thus becomes engaged in a process of self-interpretation to some degree; and where the researcher is privy to undocumented historical knowledge of the people and cultural phenomenon being studied. (Taylor 2011, 5)

I now admit that I exploited my friendship with these women to some extent. In fact, I now realise that because of my lack of knowledge of theories on the ethics of using friends as research 'subjects', in relation to the quantity and quality of data one collects from being an insider, I did not recognise the major ethical challenges (Taylor 2011). Indeed, my informant-friends often provided more information than I asked for, something I generally viewed as a positive thing, as it improved my research design as I worked to craft an original argument. Among other things, it helped me understand the complexities of living with the daily realities of South African xenophobia, something no foreigner or Congolese shied away from. I found that for these Congolese women, 'xenophobia' meant everything in their lives, starting with their struggle to settle and integrate in South Africa. For many, this included problems which were not always the product of South African hatred of foreigners. Their stories of losing husbands or male partners to South African women, or not getting jobs because they did not know enough English, could not always be tied to the hatred that some South Africans have for immigrants. The challenges related to refugee documentation, however, were common cases of xenophobia that all of us, as Congolese, have experienced, as government officials regularly mistreat non-South Africans. Others experienced it at their workplaces with their black South African colleagues. Racism was also acknowledged from white and coloured South Africans in public and in their workplaces. In fact, my participants knew, through a shared experience, that both xenophobia and racism as well as exploitation (as often we were paid less than South Africans doing the same job) were and remain an everyday reality in the kinds of jobs that refugees like us are able to do.

The following year, in 2012, I returned to my participants to ask them questions regarding the ways in which Congolese films produced 'home' and abroad spoke to their sense of Congoleseness (Vuninga 2014). I had just started my master's program at UWC where I remained for my doctorate programme. I was congratulated by my 'friend' participants, many being happy for me that I was doing '*le troisième cycle*' (as a master's degree is called in the DRC), which was already an 'out of the ordinary' educational achievement for a number of them. Men and women agreed to participate in my research. However, my research topic and questions had led me to try and balance gender as well as profession as criteria for recruiting participants. I needed to include more people involved in popular Congolese culture, mainly Congolese filmmakers and those involved in distributing films. I also engaged in long-distance – through telephone, Skype, and email – interviews with Congolese popular culturists living in the DRC and in the diaspora, including in the Americas (mostly Canada) and Europe.

The first challenge I faced with my participants, new as well as in recruiting some existing ones, was that they often had their own questions for me. They almost always asked how I managed to finance my studies. They were interested in my financial 'connections' with many assuming that I must have a full scholarship and if so, how could they also apply to get a full scholarship to begin, resume, or continue their studies in South Africa. Regardless of my seriousness in answering these questions honestly, I felt, often through their body language or rephrasing the question as if it were new, that they did not believe me. It is during this time that I felt some emotional distance slowly building up in my relationships with my research participants. However, watching Congolese films together and debating them in Lingala and Kiswahili did help in keeping the closeness often needed to get some of the information necessary to complete my master's thesis. This climate of scepticism would also inform my doctoral fieldwork in 2016 on ethnic and regional conflicts among my Congolese co-nationals living in Cape Town.

In 2016, as part of my doctoral research, I studied the tensions between Kinois (from Kinshasa) and Kivucians (from Kivu), also known as Baswahili for their use of Kiswahili language, in Cape Town. While collecting the life histories of these regional groups, balancing the number of participants from both regions of the DRC allowed me to hear a range of perspectives and to reduce the possibility of relying on one-sided information. I also employed participant obser-vation. This led me to visit (and revisit) business places, cultural, and socio-economic organisations and associations, churches, bars and restaurants as well as music concerts. At this point, I noted that most of my participants, regardless of the nature of our relationship, perceived me negatively. I struggled to establish trust and to secure appointments for one-on-one meetings as well as focus group discus-sions. When they did agree to meet me, most of our time was spent answering their questions about my finances and education. They wanted to discuss who I was, where I came from in Congo, how I became a doctoral candidate, why I chose my research topic, and what else I intended to do with the information I am collecting. I often briefly answered these questions, though in some instances I felt frustrated with the intentions behind them, which were often led by mistrust. I perceived this as an ethical concern from my partici-pants who were also worried about the presence of Congolese trans-national politics of the Joseph Kabila-era and its radical tendency especially those from the western region of the DRC (Garbin and

Godin 2013; Inaka 2016).[1] The post-2011 Congo elections has led to the rise of a Congolese diasporic activism movement characterised by what seems to be paranoia about spies and other 'intruders' working for the Congolese government operating in Cape Town. This is a legitimate concern given the efforts of the transnational Combattant (soldier) movement (and also Congolese social networks) to spread such information. The Combattant movement did not only side with the opposition by supporting the ousting of the then-president Kabila through mass mobilisations using social media, but since 2012 they have also dealt physically or verbally with those whom they assumed were Kabilists. In 2012 and 2013 in particular, one's ethno-regional identity was often the basis on which Combattants associated people with Kabilism (Demart 2013; Garbin and Gordin 2013; Inaka 2016).

At this stage, I was dealing more with ethical challenges than opportunity as I was confronted with a number of issues resembling those encountered by scholars who conducted 'ethnographic research in highly politicised environments' (Thomson 2010, 2; Thomson *et al.* 2013). Even my existing regular participants were sceptical about why I kept returning, and why I now asked sensitive questions to which I – as a Congolese of the diaspora, a Kivucian, and a 'scholar' – already knew the answers. At times, their unwelcoming or rather reserved attitude was expressed through their body language. When I was conducting a research meeting and I noted this attitude, one of the things I did was to increase the atmosphere of trust by putting most of the research

[1]   For example, in exploring Congolese transnational activities in Pretoria (South Africa) between 2011 and 2012, Inaka (2016) noted that 'Ethnicity, regionalism, and political rivalries constituted major influences on these activities. Principally, these conflicts brought into opposition Congolese from the East, who are Swahili speakers and mostly pro-Kabila supporters, (pejoratively termed *collabos*), and Congolese from the West, who generally speak Kikongo, Lingala and Tshiluba, also known as Combattants), and are generally in the anti-Kabila camp.' He continued that '[t]he rift among Congolese in Pretoria goes beyond political alignment. The rivalry also takes on an ethno-regional dimension. For example, Combattants disparage other Congolese from the East (the Baswahili). For them, it is abnormal for a real Congolese (a patriot) to support an 'oppressor' like Kabila. Thus, they consider all Kabila's supporters (mostly from the East) as Rwandans. In the course of this research, it emerged that some participants from the West perceive Baswahili support for Kabila as misplaced, particularly because the latter appears to be unable to protect them against armed groups' (Inaka 2016, 5–7, 13).

tools such as notebooks and voice-recorder aside (if I had them out already). I would then resort to an 'active listening approach' to help detect 'what was being said, or not said' through 'observing body language and nervous habits' (Thomson 2010, 30–32). And to diminish the power struggle between the participants and me, I sometimes let them control how they wanted to inform me. For example, some participants asked that I phone them instead of meeting them face-to-face, which I willingly agreed to.

This particular method needed me to have enough airtime on my cell phone to conduct conversations that were thirty minutes to over an hour long. This meant spending money I did not have, as my research was self-funded. Thus, I had to prioritise which ones of these phone-participants to interview. I had to make sure the ones I called were potential participants, so I do not waste my limited resources. But frustrations often emerged from a potential participant preferring to recommend someone else who 'knows better' about the subjects I was interested in. This, however, was another way of avoiding me. Often, the people they recommended were relatively newcomers who knew less about the period that my research sought to examine. After noting this, I would insist on an in-person meeting with those I deemed potential participants. While this often got me some of the richest information, I felt I was tampering with the 'ethical protocols' about forcing information out of people (Atkinson 2009, 27). In other instances, the Congolese I knew readily agreed to participate in my research but only because they mistook me for someone else in the fieldwork. This had its own methodological and ethical challenges too.

'I thought you were an anthropologist, or that you work for the UNHCR'

Unlike in 2011 and 2012, when people simply answered my research questions, from 2016 onwards I was suddenly confronted by a group of Congolese intellectuals who not only insisted that I explained the rationale behind my PhD research topic, but that I also explain why I went about it the way I did. In such moments, they would share with me how they conducted their own research in the DRC, their methodologies, as well as their field of study. I have encountered people of various academic backgrounds, each with their own advice on how I could approach my topic or how I was not doing what a historian should do just because I was using ethnography as my methodology. They told me anthropologists as well as UNHCR and other NGO 'agents' were the ones who do 'ethnography' and went around asking people questions on their experience.

For many of these intellectuals (most of whom graduated from universities in the DRC), historians find their information in the museums and archives or by interviewing very old people. In fact, a good number of them struggled to see what was 'past' in my 'so called' research of a history student.

In reacting to this, I was careful to say just enough to avoid being misread as showing off my 'advanced' academic skills, while answering in a way that did not sound uninformed. Furthermore, by making the answer brief I also gave myself enough time for the actual talk for which I came. I thus explained that since my research focused on the tensions between eastern and western Congolese in Cape Town, it necessitated an ethnographic approach to better make sense of 'the complex socio-cultural, political and economic environments' in which these tensions occur, and how they play out in Cape Town (Millar 2018, 654). However, my research topic and method were not the only components to raise suspicions that I could be 'working' for someone; my research skills as a doctorate student were also questioned. For example, in Muizenberg, a suburb of Cape Town, I interviewed a woman who held a *license* in history from the University of Lubumbashi. She ran a 'crèche' in her sitting room. She remarked to me that researching events of more than fifty years ago could have been better examined as 'real historical topics' (interview, 2016). She reminded me of the 'moral obligations that often confront the researcher' and the fact that I am 'most likely to do harm' if I go around asking people information that related both to the 'home' situation and led to their immigration to South Africa and their everyday life in South Africa in relation to the xenophobic attitudes of locals (Goodhand 2000, 13–14). Her argument, and I agreed with her, was that these events are happening in current time and are highly politicised and dangerous to engage with. She also referred to the increasing number of people in the Congolese diaspora who engaged in 'home' politics as well as the growing resentment between Baswahili and Kinois, and the number of Congolese spies in transnational communities and how they endangered both me and my participants. This way of policing my work is highly linked to me being from the Kivu region (the region of pro-Kabilists) who are often mistrusted by the majority of other Congolese ethno-regional groups (Inaka 2016).

In those cases where my 'anthropological method' was not rejected, my participants continued to criticise me for not doing research in the right way. For example, a different Congolese housewife and anthropology graduate from Bukavu (in South Kivu region) took me through a whole Malinowskian 'participant observation' lecture. She was clear that if as a historian I chose ethnography, then I need to do it the right way. She advised me to spend my days at the Home Affairs offices in Cape Town for at least a year and take regular notes on how they treat 'paper' applicants by asking them questions and securing interviews from time to time with both the immigrant officials and paper applicants.[2] She also suggested that I go stay with a Congolese refugee family in a black Cape Town township, such as Gugulethu and Nyanga where people are highly xenophobic toward black immigrants, and take notes and conduct interviews about this phenomenon. Her comments showed no understanding or appreciation of my research topic. I was not studying xenophobia, or the handful of Congolese who live in townships as most share neighbourhoods with middle class South Africans (Owen 2015). These remarks, I felt, had less to do with my research methodology and topic, but more with the participant's idea of what would have been best to research, how, and where.

In these two cases, I was confronted with wasting time as well as the risks of not getting the useful information I needed for my research. I chose patience, listening to their advice, allowing them to make their points, so we could then proceed with our interview. My patience was motivated by two factors. The first is that I noticed that sometimes, participants would engage in the above remarks to get in the mood of talking, to manage their nervousness toward me (mostly when they were not from my circle of personal relations), and to test my determination and set themselves in a comfort zone to begin answering my research questions. The second is that I felt that at times, these intellectuals needed to empty their chest about the kind of life they lived in South Africa despite their education. Research has already established that Congolese are among the most educated African immigrants in South Africa and yet, most of them survive in South Africa through unskilled labour such as working as car and security guards, street vendors, domestic workers, and so on (Steinberg 2005). Thus, I felt remarks such as by the history graduate woman who ran a sort of crèche in her house, to symbolise the frustrations of the many Congolese university

---

[2]   By this I mean refugee and asylum seekers, including those applying for the first time, renewing, upgrading (for example from asylum seekers permit to refugee status), as well as those appealing their rejections. (For more on these categories and how they are treated in South African Home Affairs, see Pugh 2014, 174–78.)

graduates who never got to use their graduate skills to earn a living in South Africa. Limited by the language or by foreign discrimination in the South African job market, they are condemned to beg for unskilled jobs which they share with relatively less educated South Africans and other fellow immigrant citizens. This, I felt, was behind these intellectual participants' tendency to 'mentor' me. To a considerable extent, I viewed this as a resistance towards being my mere research 'subjects'. This idea also meant they wanted us to be research partners.

In other instances, however, people readily agreed to participate in my research but only because they mistook me for an NGO agent. This often happened with men and women I identified randomly, notably street hairdressers and vendors, shop keepers, but also male security and car guards, and Congolese musicians as well as people I met at events and other social gatherings such as Congolese association meetings, funerals, weddings, and eventually, concerts. At the beginning, I perceived this as an ethical opportunity. However, it became a bit of a challenge as when I needed to follow up with them, most had lost interest in participating because I was not whom they thought I was. I thus often ended up with incomplete information which sometimes could not sit well in my efforts to craft an argument for my thesis.

A loss of trust is common among researchers conducting fieldwork 'among disadvantaged and disenfranchised groups' (Warr 2004, 758). Managing it is an ethical challenge. I understood where the idea of being an UNHCR official came from during an interaction with my tailor in Parow, a suburb of Cape Town. She told me that my questions were similar to those a woman researching for the UNHCR asked them once. The woman, I was told, assisted one of the women she interviewed in securing a birth certificate for her child after five unsuccessful years of trying. This inspired many of them to never miss the opportunity to share their refugee- and other immigrant-related problems with UNHCR agents. But in my case, there were no benefits or promises that I made to resolve their refugee-related problems such as difficulties with renewing their documents or getting documents for their families. Eventually, some lost interest in participating and worse, they discouraged others they were close to not to waste their time. Thus, I had to start again to find participants and ensure this time that I provided more clarity right from the beginning by explaining who I was and what the research was for. This approach did not secure many participants but at least the few who volunteered did so knowing that I was just a fellow Congolese woman needing help with my studies.

I still asked some of those who originally thought I was either an UNHCR or NGO agent to participate in my research. Their responses helped me make sense of their attitude towards me as a product of their varying backgrounds and frustrations related to the challenges they face in settling in South Africa. This was still helpful in filling in the gaps in my arguments based on life histories and also to theorise the limitations of my research methods in relation to how my participants perceived my identities (Gold 1958). The tendency to question and disagree with my methodology was as much about who I really was and whether the information I collected was really for just research as it was about whether my research would change their lives. While the graduates who participated in my research often understood what it meant to collect data for writing a thesis, I needed to explain to 'ordinary' Congolese that as a student researching to write a thesis, I was not in the business of changing people's lives. Indeed, it is unethical to promise to change people's lives with our research. I told them that even policy-driven research rarely results in tangible change in people's lives. Often, though, I needed to defend the rationale behind my research topic in terms of my own regional identity.

'Why did you choose to research on Kinois and Baswahili conflict?' On Not Taking Sides

The motivation for my research stems from the political feuds between the western and eastern Congolese that were aggravated during and in the aftermath of the 2011 elections in the DRC (Inaka 2016). Homeland politics shapes daily life for both Kinois and Baswahili in Cape Town, even as most focus on making a living. Thus, many questioned my ethno-regional identity to determine what motivated my choice of dissertation topic.

Congolese transnational communities, including those in Cape Town, are haunted by what Carter (2005, 60) described as 'hardening of attitude' with 'a series of boundaries'. In the field, my experience in terms of my identity can be compared to that of Chowdhury (2017, 1113–14) who explained the 'multiple identities' he experienced while researching among his countrymen in Bangladesh as 'Cambridge-educated and British'. In my case, these 'multiple identities' were present through the fact that I was not just a Congolese and doctoral candidate in a South African university. I was also an educated woman from the Kivu region. In cases when participants put my 'intellectual identity' first, my fellow Congolese intellectuals would want us to first talk about my topic choice. The challenge was bigger when dealing with those involved in 'home-land oriented activism' such as members of the Combattant movement (Caponio 2005, 938). This group of participants would first want me to explain why, out of all the 'interesting' or 'important' topics in the history of the DRC and/or its diaspora, I chose Kinois–Baswahili feuds to research. They often suggested 'better topics', such as the Beni massacre; 'genocide in the DRC';[3] the balkanisation of the DRC; the global superpowers and how they fund and sustain (armed) conflicts in the DRC to loot its resources; the complicity of the DRC government in its crisis; why there had been no elections in the DRC in 2017; and Mai-Mai and other rebellions operating in the country.[4] Others were open about their nostalgia for the Mobutu era and wished I had chosen to write the history of his 'heroism' because 'he is the best we have had so far', as one male participant in his early forties praised the late dictator. As interesting as these conversations were, they made me a bit uncomfortable especially when having them with unfamiliar participants. They were very sensitive in addition to most of them demanding profound research before validating them. For example, the issue of 'balkanisation' is one typical example of how politically sensitive engaging in this can be may it be in the diaspora.

After I explained the 'rationale' behind the Kinois–Baswahili *polemique* research topic, I was often asked to disclose whether I was a Kinoise (a woman from Kinshasa) or a Muswahili from Kivu. It often began immediately after I introduced myself simply as Rosette, 'they [would] ask for [my] second name not so they may know [my] full name but so they may identify [me] with [my] ethnicity and pigeonhole [me] accordingly', using Lumumba's (2017) words. How my identity was interpreted raised methodological and ethical concerns. Methodologically, it determined both the quantity and quality of the information I would receive from such participants. Ethically, it determined their attitude toward me, depending whether I was dealing with Kinois or Baswahili. To avoid more frustration, I

3   My research participants all knew that it had been years since over six million Congolese had died as a result of a war backed by Burundi, Rwanda, and Uganda. (For analysis see, Reyntjens 2010, 87–99; Thomson 2018b, 119–21.)

4   See for example the essay by UWC mathematician Dr Justin Munyakazi published at the Kujenga Amani Forum of the Social Science Research Council on Mai-Mai Yakutumba (Munyakazi 2018).

kept my expectations low regarding the possibility of learning from my participants during our first meeting. I knew that the first meeting would be spent letting them know about my research or my identity as a Muswahili and what it could be associated with stereotypically. I often encouraged them to talk about all the stereotypes of Congolese ethno-regional identities and often we laughed about it (Pongo 1997). Usually after this, we were all at ease and could proceed with discussing topics of my choice.

Some men tested my professional courage. They were mostly from Kinshasa and were pro-Combattants. As a Muswahili woman, asking Kinois men what they knew or thought of the feuds between themselves and 'my' people was deemed 'courageous' (for a woman from Kivu). They also viewed me with suspicion because the social media posts from members of some Congolese social networks and organisations that I am part of warned people against beautiful female spies sent to poison members of South Africa's Combattant movement. The messages (mostly voice) accompanied the pictures of the well-known Combattant signature: the slogan *ingeta*! (a Kikongo word translated as 'amen' or 'so be it'). I could therefore be anyone from a 'Rwandophone' to 'pro-Kabilist' that most Kivucians are suspected of by Congolese from the west of the country and especially those members of the transnational Combattant movement (Inaka 2016, 13; Jackson 2001, 121, 132; Reyntjens 2009, 2). Some of the participants would also ask me personal questions including whether I have ever been a victim of such feuds myself. I felt the questions were guided by their curiosity regarding my choice of topic, but mostly, what was my own position in relation to the political activities of Combattants. I emphasised my objectivity on the topics and that I was only interested in and writing about it because it has become common knowledge that there was an ongoing 'cold war' between Kinois and Baswahili. However, my position was rarely satisfactory to all as many wanted me to state my position with regards to these ethno-regional feuds.

Proclaiming myself a neutral observer of the feuds between two Congolese regional groups – one of which I belonged to – made me a hypocrite or placed me squarely on the side of the Baswahili. In the former case, the person was very careful in the ways in which they answered my research questions. Their responses were terse and cautiously chosen. I also got a lot of 'Why don't you ask your people to answer that', or the person would seize the opportunity to set me straight by defending their ethno-regional group. Occasionally, I got views that recognised and condemned these feuds by also suggesting ways for these two ethno-regional communities to live together in harmony, the dream of Congo's anti-imperialist Patrice Lumumba (Zeilig 2015).

Kivucians on the other hand often warned me against asking questions on Kinois and Baswahili feuds, as it could upset the Combattants who might be violent toward me because I was from the Kivu region. But they had a hidden agenda in their overprotectiveness, including wanting to use me as their 'strategic mouthpiece', in turn leading to the potential loss of trust of my non-Kivucian participants if they sensed I was siding with Kivucians (Blomley 1994, 31). This was mostly because Kivucians wanted to ensure that their participation in my project outnumbered Kinois so their views dominated my argument. They told me to 'tell the truth about how Kinois treat "us"'. They reminded me that I am the only historian from Bukavu, the capital of South Kivu they had ever had in Cape Town and perhaps in South Africa,[5] and that I had to use that opportunity to speak against the ways in which Combattants have been harassing Kivucians by labelling them Congolese of a 'questionable identity' and blaming them for all the post-Mobutu political and socio-economic crisis in the DRC (Nzongola-Ntalaja 2002, 229). They also wanted to use me to settle political scores with Combattants. For example, a woman from Kivu introduced me to a Kinois bouncer as her friend but who was also part of the Combattant movement and said to me beforehand; 'When you are talking to him, please explain to him that Kivucians are not Rwandans...'. And a pastor from Kinshasa I met through a friend who thought he could be the right man to speak to regarding Kinois–Baswahili feuds, asked me: 'So will you also interview Baswahili on this issue or just Kinois?' My response was simple: 'Yes, I will interview, not just Baswahili but any Congolese who can shed a light on these Baswahili–Kinois feuds; any one's view is valuable.' He then said 'When you talk to your 'relatives' [Baswahili], ask them why they prefer to associate with Rwandans than with us Kinois.'

The above caused me two sizeable 'ethical dilemmas' (Li 2008, 107). The first was the concerns of some participants, especially those from Kinshasa. Kinois, particularly those who supported or belonged to Combattants's movement, expressed concerns (or I could

---

5   I often reminded them that I was still a student. I also told them about a Kivucian historian – Jacques Delpelchin – who worked at the University of Cape Town, well known for his book *Silences in African History* (2005). None of my participants knew his work.

detect it in their body language and responses) over the fact that I could be spying on them or trying to incriminate them. Many feared I was working with human rights agencies or the South African Department of Home Affairs to build cases against them, as some were undocumented, and they could not risk criminal records.[6] The second is related to being caught up in the proverbial crossfire in the Kivucian and Kinois feuds. In this case, the major ethical challenge involved my own physical safety and emotional well-being. Researchers have already noted that 'ethical principles and guidelines tend to focus on protecting participants from harm or in some cases on empowering them', but it rarely explores 'the risks and ethical dangers a researcher may face studying certain contexts' (Piper and Simons 2005, 58). My own UWC ethics protocol clearly stipulated my responsibility to protect my participants but it did not address any ethical responsibility my research participants had to observe my safety. For example, many participants were often busy manoeuvring their smartphones as we engaged in conversations that 'trespass into areas which are controversial or involve social conflicts' (Lee 1993, 4). I often wondered if they could be recording me, especially when a person was a pro-Combattant, and what they would do with the recording if they were. When I felt unsafe, I often had to find a way to end the meeting, often by saying I had to stop for another meeting. When I stayed, I answered their questions with very brief answers, being cautious not to say things that might compromise my safety.

---

6   In a research meeting with one of the Combattants of Parow (Cape Town), I asked the man, 'Ray', about the stabbing to death of a Congolese man by another Congolese man at a club in Sea Point on Sunday 3 December 2017. This was the same night Congolese musician Fally Ipupa was scheduled to give a concert in the same neighbourhood and which Combattants had planned (successfully) to sabotage as usual. Combattants then participated in the murder, wanting to find justice for 'their' man killed by another Congolese and wanting to blame it on the musician's unwelcome concert. But another version was that both the victim and the killer were Combattants and the argument was over a R700 night shift at that club. I asked Ray to clarify that since I was told he knew the 'true' version. After he explained to me his own version of the events, he looked at me suspiciously and almost regrettably asked: 'Why did you want to know? You could be anyone sent to extract information from me...especially that the investigation is on...I am also illegal in South Africa, so I cannot afford being apprehended for anything....' I had to reassure him that I asked just to know as part of the everyday life of Congolese in Cape Town.

Conclusion

My positionality during fieldwork with my fellow Congolese moved me from being a relative insider in 2011, when I first started, to being an 'inbetweener' from 2016 when I returned to start my doctoral project. As a Congolese studying my compatriots in South Africa, I have had to deal with many challenges 'in the field' even as my participants included people to whom I am close, such as friends and neighbours, as well as participants who have become friends since 2011. I found that new participants tended to distance themselves from me, while relatively new ones (and some of the old ones) acted with suspicion as they tried to figure out who I was and what I needed from them. I also raised suspicion among my research participants because of my background as a historian and my ethnographic methods, something which participants who say themselves as fellow 'intellectuals' found strange. But my own ethno-regional identity and my gender also added to the mistrust in a diasporic community increasingly haunted by politicised identities of home. In addition, many of my participants saw my choice of research topic as both politically sensitive and 'banal'. To their mind, there were more important problems for Congolese living in the DRC and among Congolese transnationally that were worthy of research than what I came up with. In other words, my research did not prove its strength in relation to what it might contribute to better the DRC or their everyday life in South Africa. One major challenge was thus to explain how my doctoral research was different from that of policy makers.

I often explained to my participants that research is open-ended, and that I did not have answers to my research questions for them in mind. This was not only their way of testing if I was also Congolese, but also offered a way for them to assess the sincerity of my intentions as a researcher. Looking back, I see that they were testing me to learn if I could be trusted in a community characterised by paranoia about both the South African policing of immigrants and Congolese government spies, who could take any human form. This was mostly because politicised homeland identities are increasingly shaping their socio-economic networks transnationally, including in South Africa. Thus, responses such as, 'But you know the answer to that', 'But you were here when it happened', 'But you have been in South Africa for over ten years, so you know what it is like to be a refugee here', or again 'What is your own view on that?' and other remarks of the kind made me feel like they could tell I was hiding behind their voices to write about 'our' everyday life in Cape Town. It also meant that my own experience was not different and could have been enough to answer my own research questions. For this, I was continuously negotiating my fieldwork position as both an insider and outsider, leading to my becoming something in-between.

While I encountered a number of methodological and ethical challenges in my research among my co-nationals in Cape Town, I note two considerable ones. The first is the limits of field research ethics that claim to protect the safety of research participants but not that of the researcher in the field. While researchers are morally and ethically obliged to protect their participants, how participants can endanger the researcher through the ways in which they often tended to lead the 'conversations' in research meetings, and the ways in which they too 'interviewed' me, the researcher, is rarely acknowledged and discussed. As much as I tried to maintain control over who gets to ask questions in interviews, I was also willing to dance to participants' tunes during research meetings, for the sake of politeness and maintaining a climate of trust. While I was able to offer them a sense of anonymity in respecting their wishes and how I recorded the information they shared with me, the fact remains that I had almost no control over how they made use of the information I shared with them.

Secondly, studying my Congolese compatriots made me more aware of the difference between academic research and activist writing. That feeling of 'Now what?' after I had collected information from my research participants, and during my periods of participant observation with them, haunts me deeply. I am left questioning the idea that not every project can be policy oriented. My observation, as a historian, is that it is rare to read some kind of recommendations to address the issues or problems raised in most of the historians' works. The fact that I identify with my own research problems challenged me on the question of neutrality/objectivity in research. If anything, I felt that my participants were more interested in how I myself was related to my research topic, and that it is yet to fit somewhere in my writing. This is something I will continue to work on.

Further Reading

Blythe, Stacy, Lesley Wilkes, Debra Jackson, and Elizabeth Halcomb. 2013. 'The Challenges of Being an Insider in Storytelling Research'. *Nurse Researcher* 21, no. 1: 8–12.

Breen, Lauren. 2007. 'The Researcher "in the middle": Negotiating the Insider/Outsider Dichotomy'. *The Australian Community Psychologist* 19, no. 1: 163–74.

Kerstetter, Katie. 2012. 'Insider, Outsider, or Somewhere Between: The Impact of Researchers' Identities on the Community-Based Research Process'. *Journal of Rural Social Sciences* 27, no. 2: 99–117.

Moore, Jenny. 2012. 'A Personal Insight into Researcher Positionality'. *Nurse Researcher* 19, no. 4: 11–14.

5

'If they find out, we're dead': Intermediaries, Self-censorship, and Anxiety in Research as an Outside-Insider

Aymar Nyenyezi Bisoka

SUMMER 2012. I'M in a bicycle taxi in Cibitoke, one of the eighteen provinces of Burundi. It is my first trip as a part of my doctoral research, but in a location I already know. This was the same road as the one I took ten years before, a road connecting Bukavu city in eastern Democratic Republic of Congo (DRC) with Bujumbura, the capital of Burundi, via the Rwandan town of Bugarama. At that time, I was working in the development cooperation sector in these three countries. I did not yet know that these countries would later become the site of my doctoral research.

During my travels, I often found joy in admiring the meanderings of the Ruzizi River. I scanned the strips of land that stretched roughly towards the only point of intersection between Burundi, Rwanda, and the DRC. I admired this scenery whenever I visited Cibitoke. Each time, I would look at this wonderful landscape, whose glistening beauty would, paradoxically, fade into darkness as my bicycle taxi drove further away, leaving my mind to dwell on the memories of the sombre and murderous past of this part of Central Africa. Once again, that day, I realised how difficult it was for residents of this region to free themselves of the ancient scars of the past.

As we drove on this particular day, my taxi driver and I came nearer to a crowd of young people who were listening to a small object they were gathered around. It was midday. Everyone was listening to the news on the radio, as was the custom in this country. They were listening to Radio Publique Africaine, the African Public Radio, a private station that armed forces loyal to the Burundian government destroyed, in May 2015, during an attempted coup. I strained my ears, joining the rest of the crowd. The radio announced that, a mere kilometre away from where we were standing, several corpses, some tied up and others crammed into bags, had just been discovered floating in the river on the border of Rwanda and Burundi. The announcement launched the beginning of political disputes between the secret services of both countries.

Three years later, in 2015, as I was starting the last phase of my PhD fieldwork, young men known as Imbonerakure – a militia of the governing party of Burundi based in eastern DRC – decided to return home. They felt abandoned when the news of their existence had become politically inconvenient on the eve of the elections. However, they were not welcome in their country of origin. Upon their return home, they were assassinated in cold blood by the Burundian army.

When reporting this story, the Burundian press talked about a phenomenon known as the 'red berets'. 'To wear a red beret' was coded language used by the Burundian intelligence agencies to refer to the execution of young returning militia members with a bullet through the head. The story in the press had been leaked by the diplomatic corps in Kigali for strategic reasons that served both Rwandan and Congolese interests. They wanted to see the militia return to Burundi. The DRC government feared the role of this Burundian militia in the already violent conflicts between the Bafuliru and the Barundi militias on the plains of Ruzizi river. As for Rwanda, its government was weary of the alliances this militia could have formed with the Interahamwe, the presumed perpetrators of the Rwandan genocide, who had been on the run in the DRC since 1994. After the leak, it would take several more months before the news, which was in the hands of the United Nations Mission in the DRC (MONUSCO), would be confirmed.[1]

---

[1]   Author interview in Iwacu, 2014.

While these two events framed the beginning and end of my doctoral research, several other events, even more brutal and surreal, occurred. They unfolded in the provinces on the border of these three countries, the same provinces in which I was conducting my research. The violence of these events shocked, outraged, and scared me. However, at the same time I developed coping mechanisms in order to absorb it, like the skin of a bull thickens during a drought. I tried to convince myself that this violence – which is often dealt with only superficially in books about national political struggles – had not managed to permeate into the hills where I was dealing with what I conceived at the time to be less serious matters – namely, small-scale land conflicts between farmers. Yet it did not take long for me to realise that this was an illusion; the violence characterising the region was inevitably affecting the object of my research: land conflict involving local elites.

I soon learned that during the war, many farmers had lost their land and were not able to reclaim it afterwards, despite the institutions that were put in place to assist them. In my field research, I learnt that behind the land conflicts between Bafuliru and Barundi communities in the DRC, a network of arms traffickers was making big money. In Rwanda, my research examining the conflicts linked to the expropriation of the marshlands revealed that local elites connected with the governing party were implicated in land grabs and the control of trade networks through their control of the agricultural cooperatives. A network of actors was organising illegal rice sales outside of the officially recognised cooperatives. The Rwandan government suspected the Interahamwe of being behind the fraud. In Burundi, the ruling party's militia and secret service took a serious interest in the land conflicts concerning the so-called refugees. I gradually came to realise that my research was leading me onto a potentially dangerous terrain, both personally and professionally.

A Belgian professor warned me, 'Aymar, keep your nose out of these affairs.' I received the same warning from my contacts in the African Great Lakes Region. Colleagues working for local NGOs repeated the same warning:

> Aymar, we know it's important to intervene in issues of land conflicts between farmers and the elites in the region. As you work for a Belgian university, we suggest that you collaborate with [Belgian] embassies to have reliable information about the security of the areas in which you expect to conduct your research. We need to have access to the country [have permission to work in the

country], so we can't get involved [in political affairs]. We advise
you to do the same.

I began to feel that I could be in physical danger.

My doctoral advisor had warned me: 'At some point, research can
become a drug. Our search for the story may blur our perspective
on the importance of taking care of ourselves, both physically and
mentally.' But I couldn't help myself. I continued my research and was
itching to find out what was actually going on. I investigated yet found
that I was missing crucial information. It became clear to me that I
needed to be close to the very elites, involved in the stories that I was
investigating in order to obtain additional information. That is how I
started to elaborate an entire network of *intermediaries*, people who
knew the elites with whom I wanted to interact, and who could put me
in contact and vouch for my trustworthiness. This strategy allowed me
to gain a rich pattern of research data and gave me a privileged insight
into my research topic. At the same time, it presented particular ethical
challenges that I took very seriously (Nyenyezi Bisoka 2016a). However,
one notable story made me realise just how precarious the minefield
was in which I was manoeuvring. One day, one of these intermediaries
told me, when speaking of certain military elites, 'Aymar, they [certain
figures of authority in the ruling party] cannot know that he [my
informant] has told you this. If they find out, you, your informant and I
are dead.' My intermediary was referring here to some classified information regarding the death of Sarah, a farmer who had been assassinated for her land.

Throughout this chapter, I demonstrate that to conduct research
'at home' is to form relationships laden with expectations with our
informants. However, this task is more complex in contexts of war,
insecurity or 'post-war', and even more so for Black researchers whose
field of study is their own or demographically similar country. The
picture becomes even more complex when informants are political
or military elites who are difficult to access and are accustomed to
controlling and defining official discourses. The chapter discusses my
experience of using intermediaries as a strategy for overcoming the
difficulties of meeting with these elites, and for attempting to access
their hidden 'discourse'. We explore these challenges within the context
of a particular story of a woman, named Sarah. Sarah was killed in a
land-related conflict. I explain how – through the use of intermediaries – we investigated who had really killed Sarah. The article explores
the ethical challenges that come with the using of intermediaries to

understand stories of violence such as Sarah's murder. By using psycho-analytic images, the article examines the difficulties that are posed by such a strategy, especially for a Black researcher.

Sarah's Murder

Sarah was found dead on the banks of the Ruzizi river on 15 December 2014. It was clear that the staging of her assassination was organised in great detail; Sarah could not merely be found dead, but rather she had to be found assassinated. The setting had to accentuate this nuance. Her death had to be different from the others whose anonymous bodies were so often found tied up and floating in this river, the luckiest of whom were faceless, but the majority of whom were decapitated, so as to ensure their total disappearance. Everyone needed to know that Sarah was indeed dead, that she had clearly been tortured, raped, muti-lated, and, only thereafter, killed. The marks on her body had to suggest that some of her intimate parts had been brutally removed and sold to traffickers to use in initiation rites, and that she had then lived through the worst possible ordeals before dying, because she knew she could not pass to the hereafter without these intimate parts of her body.

I found a way to talk about Sarah that did not place me in any danger. My goal had never been to investigate her death in order to name the perpetrator. I simply wanted to understand the dynamics behind land grabbing, and the way in which access to land is regulated by a power that imposes itself through violence, discourse, a system of differen-tiations, and techniques of government (Nyenyezi Bisoka 2016a). But ever since Sarah's death, I have reflected on my role as a researcher: can a researcher's question, interrogate, pry into people's private lives without being held responsible for what they find? In the end, doesn't the ethical rule of responsibility compel the researcher to contribute, directly or indirectly, to a positive change within their field of study? Is this not the case especially when the researcher is working in their own environment? These are the key questions I will try to address below.

Yet aside from the staging of Sarah's body, we could overhear, spreading through the villages that neighboured the Ruzizi, 'it was partly her fault; her material possessions brought her many enemies'. Almost everyone had known Sarah, a young widow, aged 32, who had farmed the lands of her late husband who died seven years earlier and had left her with two small daughters and a son. Sarah had made many enemies by refusing to leave the land that her husband had left her and her children to some powerful entrepreneurs. Indeed, Sarah had belonged to the Barundi tribe. Although she was Congolese, Sarah had Burundian parents, as her Congolese Barundi tribe had originated from neighbouring Burundi. Moreover, Sarah's late husband was Rwandan. Sarah had thus been tied to the DRC, her country of origin; Burundi, the land of her ancestors; and Rwanda, her husband and children's country. She had owned small plots of land in these three countries and had often crossed each of the borders.

It had been easy for Sarah to farm her land in these three countries. She had been able to pass easily from one country to the other without needing a visa due to the agreements of the Economic Community of the Great Lake Countries (ECGLC) and the East African Community (EAC). These agreements regulated the free movement of goods and people. But there were other arrangements, both formal and informal, that facilitated movements for small farmers such as Sarah. She had been familiar with all of these rules, and her agricultural activity had begun to thrive.

However, Sarah's landholdings attracted the attention of several actors in each of the three countries. In 2006, Rwanda started to promote a modernised form of agriculture and decided that, henceforth, farmers' lands would belong to the state. In 2010, Sarah appealed the local authority's decision to expropriate her holdings. Meanwhile in Burundi, in 2009, the National Commission for Land and other Goods had decided that all the land reclaimed by returnees of the 1972 and 1993 conflicts would automatically be granted to them. A businessman, who was also a former refugee and currently close to the ruling party, used this political opportunity to claim Sarah's land. Furthermore, in 2011, the President of the DRC reaffirmed his wish to allocate so-called vacant plots of land to those who would be able to put them to good use. What followed was a wave of monopolisation of land by local elites, who began registering farmers' land in spite of the rights granted by customary law. Sarah lost the last remaining plots in her possession.

However, Sarah did not step aside to accept her fate; she had fought back, tooth and nail. The residents of her village all knew that she had been the victim of terrible injustice. But others also thought that the new landowners had offered her money, which she never accepted. To Sarah, her land was worth more than money, and its value went beyond its productivity. However, by fighting against those who sought to appropriate her land, Sarah had made enemies. She was arrested and tortured several times, and when the people of Karinda, her village, were asked who had killed Sarah, they often replied, 'All the businessmen who grabbed Sarah's land each had a motivation to act.' According to the farmers, it could have been the rich Burundians, Rwandans, Congolese, or even South Africans, Tanzanians, or Chinese, who were, to a greater or lesser extent, involved in the agricultural business in the three countries. Sarah had wanted to be a strong woman; she had wanted to take up a public stance, and this had been her downfall. Her killers made certain that everyone knew about her death; they wanted to ensure that other attempts of dissent or of subjectification could be silenced forever.

In 2015, I learned about what had happened to Sarah through an intermediary. In fact, I had gotten to know Sarah in the context of my research. That is why I wanted to know more about what had happened to her. But I had never been able to uncover the real story until an intermediary put me in contact with some elites, through whom I learnt what had really happened. One of my interviews with an elite actor ended with this phrase: 'Aymar, I trust you, but all of this had to stay between us [...], this information can be dangerous to you.' I was unable to sleep that night. I was scared for myself, but also for those who would henceforth be in danger because of my research. I realised that it was not just me, my assistants or my participants that could be in danger, but also my intermediaries, whom no one refers to in the literature when discussing challenges in fieldwork.

I have since then reflected thoroughly on the role of these inter-mediaries, and tried to understand two things: how does my research put them in danger? And, how might my use of intermediaries also put me in danger, as a singular researcher, that is young, Black, and Congolese? Indeed, I started doing research without realising that the research ethics were more complex than the university ethics check-lists suggested. I was not prepared enough for such a field. I could not imagine the ethical challenges behind my data access strategies (such as the use of intermediaries) and their consequences for me as a specific researcher.

Accessing Hidden Transcripts

Before starting my fieldwork in 2011, I was already aware of the need to understand the discourse of political and military elites. But at the time I was more interested in the way in which this discourse appeared in the official sphere (Scott 1990). Soon, I realised official speech often stood far from the way politics and governance functioned on the ground in the hills in which I was conducting my research. Hence, beyond the public discourse, there was probably a 'hidden discourse' that explained the political practices of the local elites.

At the time, I had just read Scott's *Domination and the Arts of Resistance: Hidden Transcripts* (1990) and I was influenced by the way in which he conceptualised resistance of subordinates beyond their practices of submission. In his view, being a subordinate, whether in a democracy or a tyranny, does imply being alienated from an ideology which seeks to legitimise the way things work. Farmers often accept constraints and submission in public, while they resist and subvert behind the backs of those in power. Hence, Scott has put forward two concepts to explain this form of resistance: the 'public transcript' – the discourse which reaffirms the power of dominant elites – and the 'hidden transcript' – the behind-the-scenes discourse that challenges this power.

Thus, throughout my research, I came to realise that subordinates are not the only ones who need to present different discourses in public and hidden spheres. Indeed, Scott (1990) states that a hegemonic ideology must, by definition, represent an idealisation, and, through this, create the contradictions that allow it to be criticised in its own words. Superiors use the ideology as a way to legitimise themselves and often seek to make people believe that the discourses and actions of those in power promote the natural order of things – natural because in line with the ideology. This is also the reason why superiors often produce double discourses; a public discourse used to reassure the subordinates, and a hidden discourse that helps to protect the status quo.

The navigation between this double discourse is what I have called the game of spheres (Nyenyezi Bisoka *et al.* 2017), a concept which allows me to distinguish between the different discourses that actors use to mobilise and legitimise themselves, depending on whether they find themselves in public or hidden spaces. The game of spheres is this strategic coexistence between the hidden and the public transcript, a way to mediate one's public face and private realities.

My study of land politics shows that the relationship between elites and violence is ambiguous. As Sarah's murder shows, the elites in the three countries are required by law not to kill, not to commit a crime, and to comply with the law. But this prescription has one exception: elites can kill and commit other forms of violence at any time they think their power is threatened. This of course leads to abuse of any type. I understood that, in these countries, sovereignty was not so much tied to the organisation and the free and unlimited imposition of state power within the confines of the constitution. For the elites, sovereignty seemed to have become the right to kill anyone trying to challenge the authority of a dominant group. It is therefore the *summa potestas* (power of life and death) that really replaced sovereignty after the 1990s in these countries. And since then, the efficiency of the state seems above all to lie in the organisation and discipline of this power of life and death (O'Donoghue 2015). The goal of the collective good that the sovereignty should attain only comes afterwards. Sarah's murder taught me that the difference between the ruling elites in Rwanda, Burundi, and the DRC lies in the organisation of this unlimited power of life or death. In short, it seemed to me that this power circulates among elites, whether in a highly centralised country like Rwanda or in decentralised countries like Burundi, and diffused in the DRC. When conducting research in countries with these characteristics, researchers adapt their discourses and practices, often unconsciously, to suit the context. But textbooks dedicated to research ethics never tell us how to do so (but see Thomson *et al.* 2013).

My initial interest in studying the elite's public transcript as expressed in public spheres moved my research towards accessing the hidden discourses of those same elites. While the public discourse often referred to the importance of human rights, good governance, justice, and so on, political practices often revealed different logics. I wanted to understand if these practices were based on a coherent hidden discourse developed by those same elites. This is how I sought to understand what had really happened to Sarah. But in order to do so, I first needed those in the field to trust me enough in order to allow me to access their hidden discourse. And for this, I had to rely on a dense network of intermediaries that I had been building up for years.

Price of Admission: Being an Inside-Insider

Indeed, from 2012 I had started to gain access to the higher spheres of society in order to gather data on the non-public discourses of local elites. In November 2012, I went into the field in order to meet with political elites and civil servants of the administrations of all three countries. My aim was to talk about the ways in which the different governments approached the resolution of land conflicts – the subject on which I had been working before becoming interested in the question of elite's subjectivity (Foucault 2001). One of my White Belgian friends, who was a doctoral student in Ghent at the time, had advised me, 'Aymar, in most cases, I find it's enough to write to the authorities to secure a meeting with them. Sometimes I just need to call and that's enough. Actually, I think it comes down to how well you present yourself. Do not hesitate to call them when you need information' (Louvain-la-Neuve, November 2011). Before going to the field, I had asked, in writing, to meet with the authorities, but my strategy was unsuccessful. Instead of waiting, I decided to negotiate my access to these high-level spheres through intermediaries. My intermediaries were for the most part people I had met, directly and indirectly, in the context of my previous professional activities, and who were, to a greater or lesser extent, close to the people I wished to interview.

I rarely knew what exactly my intermediaries had said in order to grant me an interview. I only know some of telephone conversations between my intermediary and the elite in question, contained sentences such as: 'we can trust him'; 'no, he's Congolese'; and, more rarely, 'he's like a brother'. In any case, the informal introductions often allowed me to gain access to the high-level person I was aiming to meet. At the start of each meeting, I introduced myself by saying, 'I am Aymar Nyenyezi, a student at Université catholique de Louvain (UCL) in Belgium. I'm working on land conflicts in the African Great Lakes Region, amongst other things, and I would like to speak to you [...]. I am currently writing an article about [...] and wanted to ask you a few open questions to see what you think about [...].' Because I had previously worked in these three countries in the development cooperation sector, I would always add a few words that showed my interlocutor that I was familiar with the local context. I highlighted the fact that I came from Bukavu, a city in eastern DRC, in order to illustrate how close I was to the subject and to my interlocutors.

Often, during these meetings, the interviewees, to whom I had been introduced by very close acquaintances, were very open with me, to the point where I started to wonder if I should interrupt and remind them that the information I was gathering could be used in an academic publication. However, I knew they were aware of my status as a researcher. But I also knew that they assumed I would handle the information they gave me with 'care', and would not 'break their trust'.[2] This was not carelessness on their part: my intermediary had told them that they could trust me. I therefore couldn't halt these outpourings of valuable information, as that would have been akin to saying that my intermediary had been mistaken about me, that I could not be trusted. At the same time, this insider perspective confronted me with very tough ethical

---

2   This was said to me by an intermediary, when I had asked why the authority he had introduced me to had been so open with me, to the point where he had shared information that could have jeopardised his political party.

challenges. On the one hand, I had access to certain 'hidden' discourses that were usually very difficult to gain access to. Why should I have to deny myself this advantage? Was I not a researcher whose aim was to 'know'? On the other hand, to what extent could I use the information and insights gathered?

Furthermore, during my interviews, I realised that my interviewees' trust in me was, in part, based on the willingness of my intermediaries to vouch for my character. By introducing me, the intermediaries reassured the elites that I was harmless. This meant the elites tended to give me the same trust they would give to the intermediary. For example, when I spoke to certain Hutu authorities whose families had been exiled to the DRC as a result of the war of 1972, they seemed to feel a certain degree of familiarity based on the fact that I am Congolese and Hutu. They too had lived in Congo and, in a way, we could relate to each other on that basis. A perceived common reality that was 'shared' between us enhanced their trust in me. A judge told me one day:

> Human rights? But Aymar, you know, I'm not going to tell you anything new. You know what these people [referring to Tutsi] are capable of. They started [...] in Burundi even before 1972, and now they've been in your country since 2006. You know very well how they operate and why we need to be as cunning as they are. So yes, we do talk about human rights to please the donors, but in reality, we stay on our guard (elite interview, December 2012).

The jokes they shared with me, and even, for some, the 'rather compromising information' they divulged about certain people in the political opposition, served to reinforce this identification. However, the identification occurred with elites from very different sides of the political spectrum. For example, in meetings with interlocutors who belonged to Tutsi-identified political parties, Tutsi civil society organisations, or with Tutsi public servants, identification came into play although it was of a rather intellectual kind. An interviewee told me:

> But, my brother, how do you want these people who have never gone to school to understand how to manage a country? I work with them, I know what I'm talking about. Imagine, if these uneducated highlanders from the M23 came to power in Congo, what could we expect of them in terms of good technocratic governance? Which school would they have learnt all of this at? This is

why we need to keep fighting, regardless of their legitimacy [...].
We need to use other means, like what I told you at the start (elite
interview, November 2012).

The openness of elites, their trust in me, and their assumption that I
would use the information they shared with 'care', confronted me with
very uncomfortable questions that I kept on asking myself; should I
always repeat to my interlocutors that I was a researcher, and that they
should be aware of what they told me and what not? But if I had done
that, would there have been the risk of being misunderstood and of
raising the ire of these powerful men? Would such interventions from
my side have insinuated that the intermediary who had introduced me
was mistaken about my trustworthiness? Would I have put myself and
my intermediaries in danger? What matters is not the answers I now
know. What still bothers me today is that, in those days, I did not know
how to react.

In any case, over time, my dense network of intermediaries has
become a valuable avenue for accessing hidden discourse of the elites.
My intermediaries were people of all categories: simple or powerful. I
had worked or collaborated with some in cooperation agencies in the
Great Lakes Region. Others had been introduced to me by friends.
Others belonged to my extended family. In any case, they considered
me as their 'little brother', a student of Bukavu, or a Black student
whose research could not cause them problems. This imaginary image
of a Congolese and harmless Black student was felt even more by the
elites I interviewed. Often, they began their speech by criticising the
alleged arrogance, interference and indiscretion of white scholars
before talking to me. It was as if my skin colour and my young age
automatically made me humble, legitimate, and especially, discreet,
almost silent.

So, I wondered what elites were expecting from me. This question
did not necessarily arise for the middlemen who were my friends, sat-
isfied to have provided a service. But the elites seemed to be certain
that I was on their side. Perhaps they were waiting for me to bring their
opinions into my research. But which opinion? They would not want to
hear in public what they had told me. I think they just thought I was on
their side; that when I wrote, I would manage to avoid harming them, I
would defend them. But also, I quickly understood that the data resulting from the interviews with the elites should always be confronted with
other data coming from interviews with other actors (peasants, elites
who are not recommended to me, and so on). It helped me prevent

these elites from guiding the direction of my interviews. It also allowed me sometimes to challenge them, get them out of their comfort zone, and hope for an interview full of unofficial script or 'hidden' thoughts and observations.

And so, one day, I came to know what had happened to Sarah through one of my intermediary's contacts. I had just asked a simple question: 'What happened to [Sarah]?' And the answer was as brief as my question: 'Contrary to our official discourse, it was not the bandits who killed Sarah. It was time for the farmers to understand who is in charge here' (elite interview, October 2015). Several days later, another authority added: 'It was Patrice who gave the order to assassinate that poor woman. But the party had nothing to do with it. Besides, if this story keeps attracting attention, he [Patrice] may run into problems with the hierarchy. We're going to do everything we can to stop talking about the subject' (elite interview, November 2015). It was after this particular meeting that my intermediary – who had introduced me to these contacts – told me to be as discrete as possible. He explained why Patrice would be prepared to kill us all if he ever found out that I had this information and that I could use it. I was again unable to sleep that night. Not only was I grieving for Sarah and her family, but now I feared for my life and that of my contacts, a fear that slowly turned into anxiety. Whatever it was that kept me awake, I could never speak about it very clearly, to anyone. I had to let time pass.

Intermediaries and Self-Censorship

The literature on ethical challenges in fieldwork extensively highlights the need to establish trust with one's interlocutors and stresses the importance of avoiding harm by carefully protecting one's research participants. In my case, as a researcher working 'at home', the many sources I consulted could not really address my questions about the importance, role, position, and security risks for intermediaries who introduce researchers to their interlocutors, and who play a crucial role in building trust in the field.

On questions of trust, Norman (2009, 72) underlines the need to create 'personal links' as an important step towards 'building trust and accessing the personal spheres of an individual'. In saying this, she emphasises the importance of building trust through personal connections. Norman further specifies the importance of developing and manifesting a sense of empathy towards interlocutors. Jipson and Litton (2000, 154–55; see also Ansoms 2012) conceptualise empathy as an expression of understanding, by the researcher 'of the nature of the system of beliefs, while sympathy implies the acceptance of ideology'. Whilst in the situations described by these authors, trust between the researcher and their interlocutor was established through direct interaction, this was not my case.

Ansoms (2012) takes the literature somewhat further in talking about the importance of research assistants – and highlights their crucial role in introducing the researcher within a certain sphere that enables trust building with interviewees. However, again, her analysis of ethical challenges in working with assistants does not really apply to my case. The research assistant is the one who reassures the interviewee before a meeting. However, the trust that the latter has chosen to place in the researcher remains based on a direct kind of interaction between the researcher and the participant. In my case, my intermediaries did not just facilitate access to a person, they also vouched for my trustworthiness. They put their own reputation on the line in order to convince my interlocutor of my trustworthiness. Hence, one day, the elected town councillor that I was interviewing and who did not really understand what I was doing, grew tired and told my assistant at the end of the interview, 'Frankly, I don't understand what this Congolese man wants, but as long as you understand, it's okay. Anyways, I can suppose he isn't looking to steal our lands' (elite interview, November 2011).

The level of implication of my intermediaries in establishing trust between the interviewee and myself implies a much greater level of vulnerability than a research assistant would normally face. Indeed, there is a form of identification that links the researchers, the intermediary, and the interviewee. Occasionally, the interviewee would speak to me as if they were speaking to the intermediary. I remember my meeting with a representative of an important authority figure in 2012, one year after we had first met. I can still clearly see the way in which he clasped my shoulder and spoke with such intimacy, sympathy, and familiarity. He seemed certain that I understood and adhered to the ideology of his party. Although I did not agree, I did not reply or contradict what he was saying. I restricted myself to listening and asking questions. I let him explain his vision for the governance of a country that was emerging from several decades of conflicts – a vision that I found shocking, and that he shared shamelessly because he thought that he was talking to 'one of his'.

After an hour of conversation with this man, I realised that, in an article that had been published one month earlier (in October 2012), I had included some extracts of the conversation we had had the previous year. I knew that if, by any chance, he would learn about this article, he would certainly recognise his discourse, which could potentially bring me trouble. He had the power to influence high-level authorities in order to prevent me from getting permission for my research, or even from accessing the territory. I wrote to my advisor in order to withhold an online publication of the article. But my stress at the time also made me question my judgement at having cited him (anonymously) but so directly and unfiltered in the article.

Since then, I have become more cautious and I apply a greater degree of self-censorship with regards to direct quotes or contextual details. Indeed, it is not always clear to see which information can, once it is reported, cause problems or not. Some rather banal information may reveal more than the researcher intended to the informed insider. At the same time, anonymising the narrative may take away contextual elements that are important for understanding the story. This is where the dilemma arises between serving scientific interest (to have the most interesting and concise narrative possible) and protecting the security of the researcher, intermediary, and even of the informant. With time, I have increasingly prioritised the latter. Until today, I do not know if this is the best way to act. However, I know that I am already learning, through practice, the skill of navigating a minefield of ethical risks.[3]

Sometimes I wonder if it was worth going so far in search of information that could put us in danger. Admittedly, Sarah's case seems extreme, but even so, this question is very serious for research in such contexts. It is true that, for white researchers, it is difficult to use intermediaries as I did because it is often difficult for elites to identify with them. For example, a Rwandan elite once told me, 'those whites who come to search here are often spies for their government or for Human Rights Watch or Amnesty International' (elite interview, November 2015). According to the perception of some elites, these white researchers would be there to collect information to use against governments, especially in the social sciences (Nyenyezi Bisoka 2016b). Yes, we can say that we must keep the principle of do no harm. But the reality of each researcher is more complex, which calls for their responsibility

---

[3] Let us also consider the elites we view as 'moderate', but who belong to the ruling party. I have met many of them in the African Great Lakes region. They claim to be disappointed by the system, but they think there is a possibility of fighting it from the inside. This type of person shares interesting material about resisting political parties from within, but I have chosen not to disclose certain findings in order to protect my sources.

in the choice of their field and methods. To make these choices, the researcher must try to know themselves before starting the field. They must also learn to know themselves progressively in the field.

In the case of Sarah, I will admit that I have never spoken openly of this story to anyone. Her death was staged to produce a climate of fear that reminds everyone – male and female – of their disposability at the hands of local elites and the militias they control. I had promised my intermediary to speak of it only once he had allowed me to do so, in other words when he believed that revealing the story would no longer affect his security. I considered it an ethical obligation. It is the same for several forms of other sensitive information that I had collected. These intermediaries were relatives or relatives of my relatives. They were as vulnerable as me; they are from the sub-region and do not necessarily have the opportunity to flee if ever there was a problem because of the information I received from them. They are Blacks like me, that skin colour that is a sort of border in itself when it comes to running away to save your skin and finally, they were not necessarily going to have a visa to flee if ever danger arose. I felt really responsible, ethically. So, my status as a young, Black Congolese researcher shaped my ethical obligations. At the same time, I admit that my identities – of being young, Black, male and Congolese – provided me access to the information I eventually gained.

But, in the face of the elites with whom I spoke, I did not feel this ethical obligation. I always presented myself as a researcher, someone looking for information to analyse and publish. But in the face of their openness with me, I began to ask questions and I began to be afraid that if they ever suspected that I would write about the stories that they told me, what would happen to me? But there was in me that irresistible desire to know. Being in the area, having been directly and indirectly affected by the horrors of war and violence in the region, drove me to look for this sensitive information. I even tend to think that all of this was unconscious. But I did not yet know how I will talk about it one day.

Conclusion

I may, one day, give more details about what really happened to Sarah and how she died. But at present, one thing is clear to me: I cannot say any more right now, for several reasons. It is true that my reliance on intermediaries has been and continues to be a useful technique in my research as it has allowed me to gain access to the hidden discourses of the elites. And even when I am unable to access their hidden discourse, I am at least not confronted with a refusal to meet. But this technique of relying on intermediaries requires a certain reflexivity in order to safeguard the researcher's physical and psychic well-being. For example, it is necessary to protect intermediaries. This greatly limits our use of the sensitive information we have had through them. But by multiplying the sources, their use becomes easier because they are diffused in this multiplicity.

Indeed, being introduced through intermediaries who vouch for my trustworthiness, I often gained access to information that I would normally not have done. By offering their trust to me, the researcher recommended to them by the intermediary, the elite interviewees often expected a certain loyalty in return. This was a loyalty that I had not previously consented to, and that I could neither offer nor guarantee. But at the same time, my use of the intermediary's vouching did mean that I could not simply dismiss this expectation either. In fact, we both entered into a complex 'dance' of communication in which the elite interviewee implicitly made it clear that the intermediary counted upon my discretion to not use or repeat anything potentially problematic to them, while I navigated a minefield of dilemmas on how to use the discourses gathered in an ethically responsible way.

Each time, there was a sort of mutual attraction between us, a kind of schizophrenic obsession that brought us together; the elite in his thirst to display his power-knowledge, despite the risk of being betrayed by the researcher, and the researcher in his thirst for knowledge and the fantasy of being, or wanting to be, as close as possible to the facts, despite the danger of betraying the elite's trust and suffering the consequences.

It seems that, in the researcher's case especially, this risk-taking is explained by a kind of enjoyment that comes out of the information obtained, an enjoyment that is fed and reinforced by a fantasy of getting closer to reality. This enjoyment cannot be mistaken for pleasure, as pleasure can be characterised as reasonable and tranquil, which means that one can set limits and stop ahead of a predefined barrier (Lacan 1986). On the contrary, enjoyment carries with it a force that pushes a person beyond this barrier, when even a 'risk of death' becomes part of the researchers' reality (Lacan 1986). This is what my supervisor meant when she was hinting that research was 'a drug that may blur our perspectives on risk-taking', a drug that can lead to self-destruction. This self-destruction is even more dangerous as it has a psychotic tendency. The subject – in this case the researcher – is not necessarily conscious of the alteration to their perception or judgement (Lacan 1986). Hence, the strong pull that the researcher feels in gaining access to information, and the risks that this entails (enjoyment) becomes destructive when the researcher is no longer aware of the risks they run (Ansoms and Nyenyezi Bisoka 2016).

It also seems to me that this psychotic tendency is often intensely related to a form of masochism that can itself cause additional harm. For an elite to disclose compromising information to a researcher that has been recommended to them, and for a researcher to continue to ask for information that could put their life in danger, can only be possible if this enjoyment of talking at any cost (for the elite) and knowing at any cost (for the researcher) blurs the danger that is run by the psyche and the body. In order to accept such danger, it is necessary that the image we wish to give of ourselves in these two performances (talking and knowing) is embedded in a narcissistic enjoyment of knowing that one matters. This is very likely applicable to all researchers who work in difficult and dangerous fields where they constantly put themselves in danger to access the data. As I said above, there is something more deeply related to the researcher's subjectivity and history that explains this risk-taking (Reyntjens 2009).

In my fieldwork experience, the thing that saved me from continuously expanding the boundaries on a path of risk-taking was anxiety. Anxiety arises every time I get ready to leave for the field and continues every time I come back from it, and sometimes when I'm there. It is this anxiety that makes me step back at times, to reflect on my anxiety. Although I wish that it was only grounded in my memory of the scenes of horror that I lived through during the wars of 1996, 1998 and 2004 in eastern DRC, I know that my current anxiety is no longer merely linked to the trauma of war. It is also embedded within my experiences today and within the little sentences that sometimes arise and make me bluntly aware of my own vulnerability: 'They can't know that he [my informant] has told you. If they find out, you, your informant and I are dead.'

This anxiety leads to ethical challenges or opportunities because it constantly reminds me that I face danger and that I should rethink my barriers with regards to the psychotic enjoyment I take in accepting risks within my research. This anxiety, which can impose limits on my work, can also allow me to transform a death risk into a life wish, the enjoyment of research into the pleasure of research. However, when I go back, I often relapse. I come from the *post-colony*, from these societies that have recently left behind the colonial experience, an experience of 'violence par excellence' (Mbembe 2000, 139–40). It is when I entangle myself in the 'permanent struggle against atmospheric death' (Fanon 1959, 115) that I often lose my barriers. My continuous struggle to want to know more causes me to slip into a kind of sadistic psychosis with a narcissistic tendency. I am often lost in the enjoyment, and thus miss out on the pleasure. My research, my work and, more broadly, my life then transform into a battle and obsession to – one day – find a sublime equilibrium.

Further Reading

Jenkins, Sarah Ann. 2015. 'Assistants, Guides, Collaborators, Friends: The Concealed Figures of Conflict Research'. *Journal of Contemporary Ethnography* 47, no. 2: 143–70.

Mwambari, David. 2019. 'Local positionality in the production of knowledge in Northern Uganda'. *International Journal of Qualitative Methods* 18: 1–12.

Williamson, Emma, Alison Gregory, Hilary Abrahams, Nadia Aghtaie, Sarah-Jane Walker, Marianne Hester. 2020. 'Secondary Trauma: Emotional Safety in Sensitive Research'. *Journal of Academic Ethics* 18: 55–70.

6

Looking Behind the Screen: Ethical Quagmires when Accessing Hidden Discourses[1]

An Ansoms

INITIALLY, I THOUGHT of 'doing research' as a process that could be compared to creating a kind of stage on which the researcher and the researched perform. I saw it as a somewhat artificial situation in which the researched is invited to share his/her story, discourse, or opinion with the researcher. At the same time, the researcher – through his/her scientific analysis – would give an interpretation to that story by framing it through a theoretical lens, by citing certain parts and omitting others, and by analysing it in relation to other stories, discourses, or opinions. In this view, both actors in the play know that they are part of an artificial theatre sketch and take into account how the other reads the situation.

Indeed, any researcher tries – in some way – to gain access to the participant's personal spheres by creating an atmosphere of safety and trust in which the research participant feels confident to share. At the same time, the researched also gathers information on the researcher, giving an interpretation to the researcher's perceived open and hidden agendas, and adapting his/her narrative to a particular image of how

[1] I would like to thank Aymar Bisoka Nyenyezi, Yolande Bouka, Marie-Eve Desrosiers, and Susan Thomson for their valuable feedback and deep reflections that helped me to write and improve this chapter.

he/she wants to appear.[2] As Brown (2009, 213) states, 'researchers often forget that while we conduct fieldwork, we are ourselves the object of other people's research. A variety of actors are constantly gathering different types of information on us.' The opinions based on the perceptions of the researched further impacts the research process (Fujii 2010; Wood 2006).

Researchers have written about how to deal ethically with the artificiality of the research theatre setting. How to gain consent (Thomson 2013a; Wood 2006)? How to build trust (Norman 2009)? How to interpret discourses and give priority to certain versions of truth over others (e.g., Fujii 2010; Robben 1995; Sanford 2006)? These questions have been debated at great length and in great detail by many scholars. Fewer scholars have written on the challenges of combining on-stage research life with off-stage personal life.[3] Some interesting reflections exist on the way in which both lives influence each other. But what to do when doing research is no longer limited to a well-delineated period in which data are gathered for a particular purpose, for example for writing a particular book or article? What if research and personal life increasingly merge in a long-term trajectory?

This chapter reflects upon the ethical quagmires that emerge when the researcher and researched move far beyond considering their interaction as an on-stage performance. In the first part, I present my research trajectory that brought me to a long-term engagement in the Great Lakes Region of Africa. Throughout that trajectory, the boundaries between on-stage research life and off-stage personal life have become increasingly blurred. The second part reflects upon the

---

[2]   Wall and Molinga (2008) introduces the concept of *reactive subjectivity,* to capture how respondents adapt their narratives and behaviour once they realise that they are being studied. Robben (1995) points to the importance of seduction in field research on violent conflict, used as a strategy by both victims and perpetrators. He defines seduction as a conscious or unconscious attempt by informants 'to divert us from our investigative aims by disarming our critical gaze.'

[3]   Nilan (2002) offers an interesting account of these challenges. She worked with a paid informant when doing 'undercover' fieldwork in a nightclub in North Bali; she was considered as a client whereas her informant (a young male sex-worker) was assumed to be her prostitute boyfriend by others in the nightclub. This gave her access to interesting data on local youth and the cultural constitution of health risks. She was confronted with serious problems when the rumours of her having a prostitute boyfriend spread beyond the boundaries of the nightclub into her off-stage personal life.

ethical obligations involved in getting access to people's behind-the-screen life and in people getting access to mine. Some anecdotes illustrate my struggle in handling narratives and discourses that I would normally not have had access to; and in dealing with the non-research roles that research participants ascribe to me. I reflect upon the ethical quagmires and shredded emotions embedded in my position as a cross point where people's *off-screen* stories and perspectives merge.

Blurring Boundaries between On-Stage and Off-Stage Life

I started my research in Rwanda as a young PhD student. Initially, I intended to do comparative work on post-conflict socio-economic reconstruction in Rwanda, Cambodia, and Bosnia. My intention was never to focus on one particular setting for what at that time seemed like a very long PhD trajectory. However, throughout the first stage of my research, I became intrigued by the many complex dynamics that I observed and experienced in the Rwandan countryside. Moreover, I shifted my ambition to compare socio-economic construction processes to analysing farmers' livelihoods and the impact of rural policies on their economic and social well-being. Thus, I transformed my entire research design from a quantitative study in a large-scale sample to an in-depth micro-level study that involved building up the capacity to read into people's discrete, and often hidden, discourses. Over the years, I pursued my research in six different settings, with regular returns, and built up a reputation of someone in whom local farmers could place their confidence (Ansoms 2013).

I also established connections with people who were professionally active in domains related to rural development; people in ministries, at the level of local administrations; in local and international NGOs; and in foreign embassies. I had frequent and repeated interviews with some of those people. I developed connections just like I did with my farmer research participants. However, I strongly separated my on-duty research life from my off-stage personal life. My months in the field were always extremely intense. In my head, every day had to count, and every contact had to serve the research purpose. I made a neat separation between research participants and friends and – specifically after some difficult experiences – guarded the boundary with great vigilance.

At the end of my PhD, I tried to move away from studying Rwanda. Around the time of my PhD defence, I went through the eye of a (little) storm. Rwandan authorities were displeased with my research results. At the same time, my research was misinterpreted and instrumentalised by opposition groups. Over the course of a couple of months, I got regular nightly phone calls with someone yelling Kinyar-wanda insults into my ear. And it was made clear to me that presenting my research 'on the ground' was not opportune. I moved on to working in South Kivu and Burundi, thinking it would be a step to move away from the Great Lakes Region and to other regions. Again, I became intrigued by the profoundly complex dynamics with which I was con-fronted. Moreover, after the initial fuss about my research in Rwanda had settled down, I was able and – to my own surprise – very eager to return and continue my research there.

At some point, I had an inspiring conversation with an older Great Lakes specialist scholar who insisted on the credibility of research through long-term, in-depth engagement. And at the dawn of my career as a professor, I started to gather an international team of pas-sionate PhD students around me, all active in the three countries of the Great Lakes Region. Together, we developed joint projects that allowed us to link up our research and to engage in collective field work. I decided to continue working in and on this very beautiful Great Lakes Region to strengthen my expertise on agrarian and land dynamics, and to engage in the set-up of long-term research projects in interaction with my research team and with actors on the ground.

Over the years, I have interviewed many people in Rwanda, Burundi and eastern DRC. I have elaborated strategies to establish trust, to give my research participants confidence. I've built a reputation of being serious about research ethics. I have never taped an interview but walked around with my eternal notebook, with well-formulated questions and a listening ear, with an eye for body language hinting on double layers of meaning, and with an increasingly well-trained lens to read into hidden discourses. Over the years, I refined my capacity to make people open up on their beneath-the-surface image. People increasingly shared very sensitive stories with me, despite the artificial-ity of the on-stage research theatre.

And so logically, after fifteen years of continued research in this particular region, the boundaries between that on-stage research theatre and the off-stage personal life became increasingly blurred. Brown (2009) devotes specific attention to the artificial boundary between the 'on-duty' researcher and the 'off-duty' human being. He relates how the fusion of on-duty and off-duty roles, of insider–outsider positions, and of one's identity as a person/researcher may at times be extremely challenging. And indeed, this is what happened to me. I met and connected with people over a long period. I saw them getting married, having children, I saw careers being made, and – in some cases – being broken. I saw people being happy, being sad, in peaceful times and in troublesome experiences; meeting them over and over again. And over the years, I saw them forgetting that we were performing in that artificial on-stage research theatre. I saw them ascribing other roles to me; that of the compassionate listener, the confessor, the therapist. Some people started to call me a witch, with the ability to 'read into' someone's mind. Others started to see me as a friend, or even a confidante. And from my side, although I initially tried to keep up the boundary between my on-stage and off-stage life, I noticed that it was becoming increasingly fluid in my mind as well. I started to see some of my research participants as friends and develop deep connections with them where I did not initially intend to, by giving them access to my 'behind-screen' as well.

When meeting my research participants behind their screen as well as mine, I began to access new layers of information. However, that information was not only shared with the researcher, but also with the compassionate listener, confessor, or friend that people ascribed to me. And from my side, I noticed that I increasingly began to put down my pen, close my notebook, and continue with only listening and in-depth conversations without thinking about the immediate utility of that conversation for my research. I started to engage in these relationships beyond what is expected from a researcher, maybe even beyond what a researcher is supposed to do. I developed a personal connection, and in this way, I became part of their stories, no longer as a bystander but as an active listener and reference point. I started to move beyond looking for a 'sexy' quote, or an interesting angle for my next article. However, I never stopped analysing and interpreting the discourses that were shared with me. But I never intended to 'trick' people. I realised that getting access to people's off-stage narratives brought new responsibilities.

Getting Access to Hidden Discourses and its Ethical Implications

Norman (2009, 72) points to the multifaceted character of trust, identifying how 'multiple trusts [...] may ebb and flow in the context of different individual and collective relationships'. A lot of scholarly work deals with the challenge of building up trust. Gaining trust is often a matter of getting behind the 'façade of normalcy' that is characterised by silence, secrecy, and self-censorship (Green 1995).

Nordstrom (1995, 139) argues, for example, that the louder the story in a context of violence and war, 'the less representative [...] the lived experience' whereas 'silenced stories at war's epicenters are generally the most authentic'. Norman (2009) points to the importance of emotional trust, depending upon personal relations, and highlights how building up trust may occur through intense and long-term personal involvement.

Scholars should reflect on what to do in cases where too much trust is placed on the researcher. Three essential questions emerge. First, what if the researcher gets access to discourses that he or she would normally not have obtained access to? Nyenyezi Bisoka (2016a) elaborates on this question, explaining how he gained access to the hidden discourses of Burundian elites because of the status of the intermediaries he mobilised to introduce him to his interlocutors (see also his chapter in this volume). He reflects on the ethical concerns involved in using such information. Peritore (1990) rightfully points to the difficulty for respondents to assess in advance the true extent of risks they face when participating in research, given that they often dispose of too little information to foresee the potential implications. Therefore, the researcher themselves have a significant responsibility to consider and minimise the ethical dangers (Meyer 2007) – both physical and emotional risks – to which informants could be exposed throughout and after empirical research. The researcher should be aware that despite a momentary presence in the field, the issues and discussions provoked by the research may have long-term consequences (Kuzmits 2008).

Second, what if the interlocutor imposes a role on the researcher that he/she cannot or does not want to assume? Thomson (2009a) outlines how her research on the lives of ordinary people in post-genocide Rwanda pushed her into the role of a 'therapist' which was personally difficult but gave her an insight into intimate aspects of people's lives (see also her chapter in this volume). Lee-Treweek and Linkogle (2000) point to the risks involved when researchers are pushed into the role of social workers or counsellors whereas they lack training in managing distress and trauma. Clark-Kazak (2012) wonders whether researchers can take up the role of 'social work' in her reflection on the difficulties that arose when managing the expectations of unassisted urban refugees in Kampala. Another example of unrealistic expectations is when the research participants interpret the researcher's role as that of an activist who will plead their case, or a development worker who will bring up the solutions to their problems. Thomson (2009a) refers to how her research participants appropriated her as a researcher, trying to transform her into a kind of moral 'ally' expected to defend their interests. Kuzmits (2008, 28) had a similar experience when he was 'taken hostage' for two days by community representatives who 'nearly suffocated [him] in hospitality' in the hope he would come up with solutions to their problems.

Third, what to do when intense interaction brings the researcher to feeling a deep connection and empathy with his/her interlocutor? In her TED talk, Brené Brown (2013) reflects on four characteristics of empathy: 1) the ability to recognise the perspective of the other person; 2) staying out of judgement; 3) recognising emotion in others; 4) feeling with people. Researchers' perspectives differ on the place of empathy in academic research. Whereas some argue that 'cultivating empathy in qualitative research training could contribute to facilitating more enriched, insightful research encounters' (Gair 2012, 134), others insist on the importance of staying as neutral – and objective – as possible. Lerum (2001) attempts to balance the neutrality and validity checks on the one hand, and subjective emotional engagement on the other. She pleads for engaging in emotional and subjective experiences, while keeping in mind the need for verification on interpersonal, organisational, and structural levels. As Lerum (2001, 481) concludes: 'It is thus the combination of emotional engagement with one's informants (whereby informants can demonstrate their own interpersonal power and truth) and basic empirical verification that produces critical knowledge, which is both self-reflexive and able to critique the power relations between people, institutions and culture.' However, these perspectives remain very much framed in the posture of the researcher as the professional gathering information, and not the human being engaging in deeply rooted human interconnections.

In the analysis that follows, I introduce some anecdotes drawn from the many years of research. While reflecting on the above-mentioned questions, I share accounts of people who have placed great amounts of trust in me and I reflect on my ethical quagmires in dealing with that trust. The stories are drawn from my research experience in DRC, Rwanda, and Burundi. They are deliberately left vague. The essence does not lie in the details of the account, but in the ethical questions they raise.

Let us go back to the first question. What to do when I gain access to narratives that I would normally not get access to because my interlocutor forgets about the fact that we are both performing (or meant to perform) on a research theatre stage? I often think of a paper I read many years ago, in which the researcher gave an account of how he would invite his research participants into a bar to share a lot of alcoholic beverages in order to gain access to their hidden narratives. I felt profoundly disgusted by his boasting about his high alcohol tolerance as an important asset in his research design, and his lack of any remorse for having tricked people into forgetting that they were performing on a research stage.

However, I occasionally wonder whether I am not doing something quite similar. I have the capacity to make strong connections, and I frequently do so during my research – and other – encounters. What to do when people look me straight in the eyes and we build up a connection that goes beyond the theatre of researcher and researched? As the years pass, this happens more and more often. I get access to people's behind-screen life. What to do with the narratives I gather when my interlocutor starts to see me as an insider and shares things with me that he would normally not have shared? It is extremely hard to determine which parts of those narratives I can still use as 'data', and which parts are part of private encounters in which my interlocutor assumes that I've stepped outside of my research role. I once told one of my interlocutors: 'The researcher in me liked you way more when we weren't friends yet. In those times, I could freely use the quotes I got from our conversations.'

And what to do with narratives that I gain access to because people put excessive amounts of trust in me? Whereas in the beginning of my research, it was very hard to get access to politically sensitive information, this became increasingly easy over the years. In one of my research settings, I stumbled over a very problematic situation that involved well-connected, high-level political persons. During my time in this setting, our focus groups would frequently be interrupted by the sound of the motorbike of an agent linked to those elites. One day, one of my focus group participants shouted out: 'Gosh, does he really think he can intimidate us like this? Does he really think that this stupid sound will prevent us from telling you the whole story? An, we know you. You have been here many times before, and despite all the things we told you, nothing bad ever happened. We know you will be able to tell this story and that nothing bad will happen to us.'

I spent several weeks investigating, gathering information on all the details of the story with a variety of research participants. I checked and cross-checked the facts and narratives. However, I also started to realise that the story was sensitive, and if traced back to the setting, the consequences could be problematic for the whole environment. I also started noticing that it would be very difficult to sufficiently anonymise the story. I even organised focus group discussions with my informants to reflect together on how to do that. Many of them were eager to know that the story would get out. However, they placed huge amounts of trust in me, assuming – on the basis of our previous interconnections – that I would be able to tell their story in a way that no harm would fall upon them. In the end, I realised that I could not guarantee this, and so decided to not get the story out. The data are still burning in my computer, and I know that many of my research participants would be profoundly disappointed to know that they shared all that time and took all that risk to contribute to a research project that never led to anything.

This brings us to the second question. What to do when informants share information with me because they see me as an activist? What to do with informants who hand over sensitive information and place their trust in me to use that information for what they perceive as what should be core to my scientific mission? In 1966, Beecher, while commenting on the article 'Ethical and Clinical Research' (Beecher 1966), describes how the researcher 'sometimes finds himself in the middle of an active political arena, that none of his informants accepts his plea of scientific neutrality, and that each tries to enlist and monopolise his support'. However, one could go way further, and wonder whether there is anything such as scientific neutrality. The decision to analyse or not analyse certain questions is already a form of taking a position. I know that I have profoundly disappointed people. Some of my informants feel betrayed because of my retreat into what I define as my research role. One person once called me a 'lame' researcher. Another person – in a frustrated reaction to my refusal to write about a particular topic – highlighted the role of those 'so-called researchers' who only shout about how right they were, when the dust settles after the bomb has exploded. He warned me that on that day (adding 'if I'm still alive'), he will remind me about his words and my hypocrisy.

I feel similarly awkward when informants ascribe to me the role of the therapist. However, given the nature of our team's research, it would be hypocritical to radically refuse this therapist role. The very nature of our research triggers people to talk about very intimate aspects of their lives: the (land) conflicts they are involved in, and the impact this has on their social relations and personal well-being. At the same time, experience has taught me all too well that I am not trained to deal with people's trauma. Moreover, my engagement as a researcher does not allow me to provide a long-term follow-up on the emotions that my questions may bring up. So I have to be extremely careful in reading well how far I can go during my research encounters. The theatre methodology that my team and I have developed in order to talk about land conflicts is one way of dealing with this challenge. Informants often feel much safer to reflect on the consequences of land conflicts when connecting their reflections to a fictive theatre sketch instead of their own lives, although, again, there are many ethical reflections to be made.

Turning to the third question, what to do with the deep interconnection that certain research participants and I have built over the years? This is particularly challenging since my emotional engagement in the field led me in either direction of the political issues and debates that shaped the context of my field work. Sluka (1995, 287) observes that 'when conducting research based on participant observation in communities involved in political conflicts, it is generally the case that [...] no neutrals are allowed'. The same goes for research in the Great Lakes Region; researchers are compelled to take a position on the political issues and debates despite the will or intention of the researcher. However, over the years, I have frequently interacted with people from very different sides of the political sphere, some of whom become good acquaintances and others whom I consider friends.

At times I feel shredded by the inherent tension between their stories and perspectives, and the empathy that these sources raise in me. How should I navigate empathy when a high-level politician confessed to me how he understood his life to be in a gilded cage, in that he compromised his personal values in exchange for political loyalty? I listened to a very honest self-understanding of how he let himself be driven away from the principles that once inspired him to enter politics, and I saw the sincerity of his desire to nonetheless continue to be guided by those principles in some of his political actions. How should I reconcile this empathy with my compassion for the civil society actor – and long-time friend – who confessed to me the very next day how tired he was about being chased by his closest political ally? How do I frame the threats he faces for his undoubtedly useful work? And how do I react when one day, such a person calls me to say that he is running for his life and asks for my help? How should I react the day he arrives in my office and hugs me because he survived?

I sometimes feel that research is the point in which people's stories and perspectives align. Those stories and perspectives are shared with me because of the great level of confidence and trust that people place in me. However, I often have to be extremely careful about sharing my information with them. Research ethics are fundamental in my role as a researcher but also in my role as the acquaintance, confessor, or friend. I have to safeguard at all times against ever passing on sensitive context-specific information from one side to the other. Wood (2006) reflects on the unintended consequences of sharing her experiences with local 'friends' or passing on information confidentially to a responsible person that may 'make a difference.' I am acutely aware that such unintended consequences could lead to very problematic – and unethical – intrusions in people's lives.

However, my safeguarding against sharing any sensitive, context-specific information from one side to the other results in messy situations. To cite a friend: 'Don't you trust me? [...] You look at me as a friend, but sometimes as ... a subject. My look at you is cleaner ... and [more] innocent.' He took my lack of openness as a lack of trust. His disappointment is a logical reaction to my refusal to talk about a specific case after he gave me an insight into his off-screen narratives. Several people have hinted that I would make a good spy. Someone once told me: 'You give someone the impression of being very open and transparent, but actually, you haven't disclosed anything. You are like a complex movie of which I only got – and will ever only get – to see the trailer.' People sometimes ascribe double layers to my identity, layers that I don't feel comfortable with, interpretations that are by no means close to what I want to be myself.

Others interpret my ambiguity differently, such as the friend who once told me: '[Your capacity to read into people] is a gift. You use it with your heart wide open, which means that you use it well, you use it to achieve something good.' Another friend shared 'I like you for the way in which you do the things you do.' When I replied to him that he doesn't even know what I am doing, he responded 'exactly, and that is the very reason why I like you. I trust your judgement.' A huge amount of responsibility and trust that both have placed in my hands, blindly assuming that I will be able to handle it well....

Conclusion

Nilan (2002, 368) describes how 'the researcher as a human subject is [...] in flux, dealing constantly with shifting realities and contradictions.' Dealing with those shifting realities and contradictions is a profoundly complex ethical journey. I carry the weight of many people's secrets in my heart. I am a researcher, and many of those secrets have been shared with me in my status of researcher. However, very often the persons involved shared those secrets not just with the researcher in me, but also – and probably more so – with the compassionate listener, confessor, therapist, witch, friend, or even soulmate they saw in me. And I have to assume the weight of those secrets. Those roles were not roles that I initially chose to print on me when I engaged in building up a connection with those persons. However, throughout the years, for them as well as for me, the boundaries between research and 'real life' got blurred on both sides. This comes with new responsibilities and ethical challenges that are very different from those traditionally discussed in the academic literature. Nonetheless, these challenges are very real and shape the way in which I evolved as a scholar, but also, and more importantly, as a human being in interaction with other human beings.

Further Reading

Fujii, Lee Ann. 2010. 'Shades of Truth and Lies: Interpreting Testimonies of War and Violence'. *Journal of Peace Research* 47, no. 2: 231–41.

Norman, Julie. 2009. 'Got Trust? The Challenge of Gaining Access in Conflict Zones'. In *Surviving Field Research: Working in Violent and Difficult Situations*, edited by Chandra Lekha Sriram, John C. King, Julie A. Mertus, Olga Martin-Ortega, and Joanna Herman, 71–90. London: Routledge.

Nyenyezi Bisoka, Aymar, An Ansoms, Koen Vlassenroot, Emery Mudinga and Godefroid Muzalia. 2019. *Le Serie Bukavu: Vers une decolonisation de la recherche*. Louvain-la-Neuve: Presses Universitaries de Louvain.

7

Scholar-Activist?
On Relational Accountability
and an Ethic of Dissemination[1]

Susan Thomson

Your writing is so important to us. It gives us hope. To know that someone who is not a Rwandan understands the country like we do is a gift. You are a true activist because you are not afraid to say what so many Rwandans cannot say – that the RPF has politicized the genocide and our history. Thank you for your work. Please keep writing. We need more foreigners to be a 'voice of the voiceless'.

– Rwandan human rights activist,
introducing me at an event in Canada, April 2011

BEFORE I PUBLISHED my first book in 2013, dissident Rwandans living in parts of Europe, Canada, and the United States saw me as a scholar-activist. I was 'true' because they thought that my research findings – which critiqued the post-genocide policy of national unity from the perspective of thirty-seven rural poor – overlapped with their political aspirations to unseat the current government. They

[1] An Ansoms, Yolande Bouka, Marie-Eve Desrosiers, Annie Getz-Eidelhoch, Rosette Sifa Vuninga, Jade Roxburgh, Shelagh Roxburgh, and Tammy Wilks provided thoughtful and engaging feedback on various drafts. While I was unable to incorporate all suggestions, I am grateful for the exchange of ideas.

saw me as an activist because I used my academic platforms to share my findings with non-academic audiences through media interviews, opinion editorials, and from 2010, via social media platforms such as Twitter. While the mantle did not sit well with me, I did not challenge their framing of my scholarship as 'activist'. Indeed, as a white academic raised and educated in Canada, I did not give my activist standing a second thought, even as I spent time working with Rwandans in the diaspora, helping them write press releases and policy briefs on political issues of importance to them, and later, writing affidavits to support the asylum applications of Rwandans seeking to leave the country. Others considered me an ally because the government had shuttered my research in August 2006, claiming it was against ethnic unity. The Ministry of Local Government officials soon ordered me to participate in a citizenship re-education camp, something I did to protect the identities of the rural people I consulted as part of my project (Thomson 2009a; Thomson 2011).

When Rwandans in the diaspora learned about my forced re-education, many expressed dismay upon learning that I had been treated roughly 'like us [dissenting] locals', and that I now knew what 'it felt like to be a target of the government'.[2] I failed to fully appreciate what my experience of being forced to leave Rwanda meant to them, and how this shaped their expectations of me. Many of the handful of Rwandans who saw me as an activist/ally had self-exiled, citing a lack of political openness and the pressures of living under the post-genocide government, the Rwandan Patriotic Front (RPF), as reasons for their departures. At the time, I did not fully understand that the exiled Rwandans who made use of my research saw me as a sister-in-arms to their political activism, even as I willingly shared myself with them. Instead, I considered myself a scholar who was simply reporting my findings and sharing my difficult fieldwork experiences as openly and honestly as I could. After all, I thought, sharing one's findings on multiple platforms, packaged for different audiences is the work of academics – it could hardly be called 'activist', could it?[3]

---

[2]   Email correspondence from 2012 and 2013, both on file with the author.

[3]   As I navigated the responsibilities of activism, it bears noting my structural privileges as a white, fully-funded, Canadian, female political scientist. To my mind, there are fewer career penalties on white academics, who generally get a free pass to pursue the questions we want in the locations we wish to study. My work also benefited from a qualitative turn in political science, eschewing strictly positivist epistemologies and methods that dominate

It is the journey of realising the importance and impact of my work for Rwandan political activists and human rights defenders that animates this chapter. If an ethic of dissemination exists, then it should be woven into the research process, rather than functioning as a by-product of the circumstances of writing up and publishing across platforms. Was I, for example, wrong to assume I could use the life histories of the rural farmers in my interview sample in non-academic publications? I certainly did not explain all the products that the stories of my participants could be used in; indeed, I did not foresee the need. I soon became a foreign academic of interest to some Rwandans in the diaspora as I could say and write things they dare not, and my re-education experience actually put me on the map, so to speak, as a critic of the government, even as my project was not designed as such. While I could not have anticipated government interference in my project, my experience raises useful questions to think through the *how* and *why* of dissemination, as a product of a series of working relationships: both with the rural Rwandans who agreed to participate in my research, as well as those politically active Rwandans living outside the country who seek to influence politics at home.

In this chapter, I argue that consciously centring our relationships matters as it serves to remind social scientists to regularly and rigorously interrogate our own research practices and our structural privileges during write up and publication. I do so as part of calls within political science for greater reflexivity, something I understand as 'a keen awareness of, and theorising about the role of the self in all phases of the research process (Schwartz-Shea 2006, 103. See also Fujii 2016, 1150–51; MacLean *et al.* 2019). I also draw on feminist ethics to think about how to represent the 'other', to reflexively engage issues of power and control over whose voices are prioritised, how their voices

---

the discipline. I also believe academics have a responsibility to share our findings with policymakers and practitioners (Thomson 2009b). Lastly, I enjoyed a level of professional gravitas as someone who had conducted, in the words of my external examiner, 'brave and courageous' work. As such, my experience of scholar-activism is different – structurally, practically, and personally – than colleagues who, unlike me, intentionally chose the path, something social scientists have prescriptively analysed. See, for example, Pulido 2008; Suzuki and Mayorga 2014 as well as guidance specific to 'Africa' from Abrahamsen 2003; Mama 2000; and Nolte 2019.

are rendered, and for which audiences (Hill Collins 2013; Stern 2006; Thomson 2018b). I offer my experiences as a form of autoethnography, to situate my personal and anecdotal experiences of Self as part and parcel of what we know and how we know it (Akello 2012; Davis and Breede 2015; Roxburgh 2017). I contend that doing so improves our ability to contribute to knowledge by making plain the messy and sometimes contradictory relationships that frame our research process and its many products (books, journal articles, conference presentations, op-eds, blog posts, and such).

In acknowledging the messier, hard-to-manage elements of writing up, we can also see that our findings will be read, interpreted, and even politicised in ways that go beyond the ethical commitments we made to those whose stories and experiences fill the pages of our publications (cf., Johnston 2010). As much as the discussion that follows is a product of my particular experiences and positionality, the broader narrative of how our research is received after publication holds lessons for other scholars, to model how I mediated my primary ethical duty – of protecting those 37 Rwandans who trusted me to tell their stories – with the expectations of some politically engaged Rwandans who found resonance in my findings, and the missteps I made in my urge to 'give back' to the people and communities that made my research possible.

I thus modestly propose a framework of relational accountability in research. In so doing, I offer a reflection on twenty-five years of work in and on Rwanda, of the many missteps of doing research and to highlight that academic life is a process fraught with contradictions and paradoxes that scholars must embrace in all facets of our post-fieldwork life (writing, speaking, teaching, and mentoring/advising). This embrace must include soul searching about the hubris of what academic research can actually accomplish, what it means to speak with, and not for, our research subjects, and whether or not speaking with is 'activism'.

I advocate for an acknowledgment of relationships as a series of living, relational commitments that reside at the heart of ethical practice, not behind the myth of scholarly detachment or objectivity. I am hardly the first to suggest an embrace of the emotional. Feminists and other critical social scientists have long advocated for researchers to be fully human (Hale 2008; Hesse-Biber 2014; Parkinson 2019). I am far from the first to propose that researchers embrace ethics as an ongoing responsibility and not 'a discrete task to be checked off a "to do" list' (Fujii 2016, 727; Millar 2018; Nordenhaug and Simmons 2018). What I do differently in this chapter is to extend the notion of possessing an ethical sensibility in write up and dissemination that is informed by how readers and other end-users of our research understand the politics and positionality of the researcher as well as the sociopolitical and cultural climate of 'home' (being the place under study).

To make my case, I introduce a framework of relational accountability, rooted in indigenous ontologies (Smith 2012; Wilson 2008). I draw on this scholarship to explain that the social world can only be understood through relationships, and that researcher accountability to all of our relations underpins our topic selection, research design, methodology, modes of analysis, and interpretation, to whom and how we present our findings. I then turn, in the second section, to discuss the ethical balancing act of being 'a voice for the voiceless', something I initially understood to be about my positionality rather than a series of relational commitments to different audiences. In this section, I examine if scholars risk an abandonment of consent protocols and other ethical commitments when external actors ask us to participate in non-academic activities and publishing. Do we have ethical duties to readers and other end-users of our research findings that go beyond what we promised our research participants?

These are questions that have come up for me as I continue to write about Rwanda since the 1994 genocide, working from the qualitative interviews I gathered in 2006 and updated with Rwandan researchers in 2016 (Thomson 2018a; 2018b; 2020). They also emerge in my advising and mentoring of graduate students working in African settings, most of who are based at universities in African countries. I have no firm answers as my overarching point is that research is a process, not just a product. I consciously choose not to provide a conclusion to this chapter, something some readers may perceive as a cop-out. My aim is to encourage readers to use my theorising of Self as a framework for reflection rather than provide a list of prescriptions based on my specific experience. As such, readers can utilise the framework of relational accountability through my process – rather than my endpoint – to allow others to link my reflexive, interpretative observations to their own research projects. As an interpretivist, my approach to research includes both a commitment to a reflexive process of self-scrutiny as well as an appreciation of what some people think and do, what kind of sociopolitical problems they face, and how they deal with them, to understand and explain what is meaningful to whom and why (Fujii 2010; Thomson 2013a, 14). Given this stance, I hope my experience can help other scholars whose work is received (and perceived) as politically charged to reflect on, and perhaps learn how to navigate sticky situations when they arise.

Relational Accountability

Accountable to Whom?

Research is about unanswered questions, and as Wilson notes (2008, 6), the research questions we ask also reveal 'our unquestioned assumptions' about the world we study. If we accept this premise, then research is also about why, how, and with whom we conduct research. In my case, there was no question in my mind that I would conduct doctoral research in Rwanda for reasons I set out in the Preface to my 2013 book on reconciliation since the 1994 genocide. I wanted to explain to my readers that I had been working *on* Rwanda since 1994, to lay bare my relationship to Rwanda and Rwandans. I did not really start to do my research *with* Rwandans until 2005, when I began drafting my dissertation proposal as a requirement of my Canadian PhD programme. This distinction of 'on' and 'with' matters, for it was the intellectual and personal work of writing my proposal and the accompanying institutional ethics application that made clear the relationships that my research would need to be successful. In all honesty, my measure of success was self-serving, as the research would result in my doctoral degree. 'Success' was gathering the field data needed to write my thesis. As much as I thought my pre-fieldwork writing had centred the relationships I would need to develop with Rwandans, the truth was that those relationships were instrumental, insofar as I needed people of different talents and roles to complete my research.

In my focus to meet the minimum requirements of good ethical practice, framed by Canadian federal law on research with human subjects, I placed the Rwandans who worked with me during the course of my doctoral research in a series of service roles without fully realising that these are relationships to which I am also accountable: research assistants, translators, drivers, and, most importantly, interview participants as well as a range of state agents, including ministry representatives, local government officials, police, and soldiers (the individuals Nyenyezi Bisoka calls intermediaries). Let me be clear; I did not take my ethical responsibilities lightly and I did the best I could, given the context in which I carried out my ethnographic work. I also recognised that my primary responsibility was to those Rwandans whom I interviewed, where trust, confidentiality, and humility informed my every encounter. I also include in the list of relationships I nurtured, and for which I am thus accountable, those where I was the weaker party, with, for example, the local government officials on whose good will and permission my research depended. My early publications focused almost exclusively on the ethics of human subjects' research with vulnerable and marginal populations (Thomson, 2009a; 2009b; 2010; 2013b. Cf., Lake *et al.* 2019).

But my early work neither considered the politics of dissemination, nor the extent to which research is not possible without a sincere engagement with people, and that being accountable means recognising both what motivates our research while also appreciating that people will react to us as a (temporary) presence in their lives in different ways. Most importantly, accountability also means holding true to ourselves as the primary instrument of research, and to uphold the commitments and promises we make to those who make our research possible, while being mindful to not promise more than we can truly deliver. It also means recognising that our presence in the field site may linger long after we leave. In Rwanda, I found myself in relationships with people who did not feature in my research proposal or ethics applications – government officials and the local police in particular. Yet, it soon became clear that I was also in relationships with them, for I needed their tacit consent to simply visit rural hillsides, where I met and interviewed most of my research participants.

Accountable How?

What would take me more time to figure out and begin to write (and teach) about was the extent to which my doctoral work was reflective of my personal politics, insofar as I sought to foreground the post-genocide experiences of poor rural Rwandans, as a way to understand and explain the power of the Rwandan state before and since the 1994 genocide. At the time, my personal politics did not extend to activism, as much as I was working to know Rwanda from the perspective of ordinary people. It was not until Rwandans in the diaspora staked a claim to my findings that I started to think through the relationships I had with those who used my findings for their own purposes, purposes I sometimes did not agree with or even respect. I do not think I would have changed my research topic or design had I known of the activist expectations of some Rwandans in the diaspora. Indeed, I doubt it is at all possible to anticipate how our research findings will be read and understood by different audiences, but I now think that researchers can assume, in the age of social media, what the public uses for our findings are. In assuming public use by local activists, we can think more deeply about how we write up, noting the larger political and social world in which our work, and the Self, are embedded, to consider whether and how our findings may be politicised, to what end, and by whom.

Having one's work politicised is not a bad thing *per se*, for we too exist as social and political actors. I proffer only that we researchers have a duty of care to our readers, for we are also in a relationship with them. Sometimes, such relationships will become personal, resulting in a measure of relational accountability. This means that we need to find a way to navigate them that honours the research process, protects the people whose stories fill our pages, while also recognising that our findings may become a vehicle for political change, even when we do not intend as much. In my case, Rwandan activists used my research to demonstrate that the RPF governed without regard for human rights, and that it was using the language of reconciliation to consolidate its political power.

In my case, an ethic of dissemination would have perhaps been more obvious to me had I considered the political nature of my project, beyond what I thought was my core audience: other academics and Western policymakers. I knew my project was political insofar as I knew my foregrounding of the experiences of violence of ordinary people, before, during, and after the 1994 genocide as a valid and knowable form of knowledge ran counter to mainstream social science, where local, bottom-up knowledge hardly matters (Harding 1991; Mügge *et al.* 2018). Working from the so-called margins of society, to understand the lives of people subject to the authority of the state was a political choice (Rutazibwa 2018). Had I been more self-aware about the relationships to the Rwandans who would come to use my research, and the responsibility of accountability I now realise I owe to those who made my research possible, I could have better understood my ethical duties as arising out of relationships, even those I did not foresee or with people I did not particularly like. My ethical shortcoming at the time was my failure to appreciate the nature of the relationships that make our research possible; we fail to understand, and thus explain, how our presence in their lives informs our research findings (Lake *et al.* 2019). We must remember at all stages of research – design, implementation, write up, and dissemination – that our work is far from value neutral. In choosing a particular topic, method, mode of analysis, and dissemination, we reveal our understanding of the political and social context in which our research is situated. Critically, our understanding of the research environment does not end when we inevitably leave the field site, to return to the relative safety of our desk to write and publish.

Personal Experience and Sociopolitical Understanding

In April 2006, I started my field work in southern Rwanda, settling in Butare (now Huye) town. I had been preparing to start my research for at least a decade. I first visited Kigali, the capital, in late March 1994, as a young United Nations staffer. As I write in the Preface of my first book (Thomson 2013a, ix–xxi), I arrived in Kigali just ten days before still-unknown persons shot the aircraft of then President Habyarimana out of the sky. The downing of the presidential aircraft is widely believed to be the event that sparked the start of the 1994 genocide. It also marked the resumption of Rwanda's civil war between the government of the day and the then rebel RPF. By 12 April 1994, Hutu hardliners had seized control of the state, with government-sponsored militias fanning out to oversee the extermination of ethnic Tutsi. The policy of genocide implored ethnic Hutu to kill their Tutsi kith and kin. Many did, with an estimated 200,000 Rwandans participating in the deaths of at least 500,000 Tutsi (Des Forges 1999, 15–16; Straus 2004).

In July 1994, the RPF rebels ended the genocide, taking political power under the guise of power-sharing. By 1999, the new RPF government would handily control the government, the military and civil society, as it sought to remake Rwanda in its vision: a modern society where Rwandans work together to develop the country, free of ethnic division (Thomson 2017; 2018a). This policy of forcible reconciliation captured my interest, as the RPF leadership implored Rwandans to eschew the ethnic identities that they believe drove the violence of the genocide. The individual killings that culminated in the Rwandan genocide touched everyone who lived in the country as 'it was a hill-by-hill, home-by-home thing' carried out with machetes, hoes, and other everyday implements (Prunier 2011, 1). The genocide became part of daily life, a permanent imprint on all who were in the country at the time. It was the intimacy of the genocide that drove my doctoral project. I wanted to know how ordinary rural people were faring since the violence of the genocide ended, as some eighty per cent of Rwandans live on rural hillsides.

In my wonder, it did not really occur to me that maybe I should not have been able to work in parts of rural Rwanda among impoverished, war-affected people. In not stopping to consider if I could ethically and practically conduct research, I failed to fully acknowledge my structural privilege as a fully-funded doctoral candidate, for whom going to 'the field' was assumed. As Fujii (2016, 1149) notes, 'just because funders, Institutional Review Boards and dissertation supervisors have given the project the "green light" does not give research automatic "right" to intervene in people's lives without consideration the power implications of what they are doing'. Of course, no one in Rwanda was obliged to speak to me about their experiences of violence and reconciliation. Still, I approached the process of gaining consent carefully and systematically, for my primary purpose was to emotionally commit to, and show respect for, the Rwandans I studied, in full recognition that the relationships I formed with my research participants would be emotionally challenging, but that these challenges would provide the necessary backdrop to provide a detailed ethnographic account of social and political life since the 1994 genocide (cf., Chakravarty 2012; Skjelsbaek 2018).

So, I proceeded, relatively confident that I was prepared. After all, I had been visiting the country since 1994, had invested in learning the local language, Kinyarwanda, found local organisations to sponsor my project, and had received all of the necessary permissions from the government. I consciously assumed a feminist posture of supplication, meaning I sought to build reciprocal relationships with the Rwandans who participated in my research (Berlant 1997; England 1994; Kobayashi 1994). It also meant that I had assumed, as a part of my reflexive approach to field work, that the Rwandans who agreed to speak with me held greater knowledge than I ever could. As such, I opted for life history interviewing as my primary mode of learning from Rwandans. I also thought that supplication would minimise the asymmetrical power relationships that defined my field work. I should have realised that the minimum standard of reciprocity, of relationships rooted in mutual respect, trust, and empathy was near impossible, given the vast chasm between my white, upper middle class, east coast Canadian self and the lives of poor rural Rwandans whom I consulted. In other words, researcher sensitivity to the power relations that shaped my relationships with a handful of rural Rwandans does not – and indeed cannot – erase or negate them; and that there is really little that can be done to reciprocate, with pen and paper, their presence in my research.

Relational Vulnerability

In my focused efforts to meet the bare minimum of good ethical practice, I failed to fully recognise the human pain and social costs of surviving mass atrocity, something I came to understand as a form of ethical loneliness (Schulz 2018). For me, ethical loneliness operates as a reflexive position to help me interpret Rwandan political life, as I had few people in my early professional life on whom I could lean to discuss and process my interpretation of what Rwandans had gone through, the violence they experienced and the herculean efforts they had to undertake to return to normal life.[4] As many Rwandans told me, there was no going back to normal. Optimism, they said, was something that belonged to government officials. Almost everyone I met – survivor or perpetrator, young or old, rich or poor – felt some form of abandonment by family or neighbours as well as from their political leaders and the administrative system that expected them to reconcile with self and others. My presence likely added to this sense of loneliness and abandonment, since research offers no way to change the lives of those who make it possible.[5] A sense of making do, of barely getting by, characterised my entire project. I would only begin to appreciate the weight of ethical loneliness once I started publishing, as I wrote about how and why the government of Rwanda had stopped my research. I did not consider my project a failure, even as the experience of having my doctoral project interrupted came to define, in my mind at least, how my work was received by academic peers and Rwandan exiles, something I discuss further in the next section.

When representatives of the Ministry of Local Government stopped my research in late August 2006, claiming that I was wasting my time talking to ordinary Rwandans about national unity initiatives, since they were 'liars' who did not appreciate all that the RPF was doing for them, I was not thinking about publication when my work was stopped (Thomson 2011. See also Thomson 2009a; 2013a). I only wanted to figure out how to protect my interview material and safeguard the identities of the rural Rwandans who participated in my

4   Although I did develop at the time some close professional relationships with other foreign researchers working in Rwanda, including Alison Des Forges, Marie-Eve Desrosiers, Lee Ann Fujii, Catharine Newbury and David Newbury, among others.

5   Many of the Rwandans who consented to participate in my project knew I would 'hold their secrets' and in hopes that 'storms' like genocide would not befall their children (Jeanne quoted in Thomson 2013a, 3).

research. As far as I know, I did successfully protect them, something I partially attributed to my own understanding of the sociopolitical context at the time as well as my careful management of interview data (Thomson 2010; 2013b). As I packed up under the watchful eyes of government officials, leaving the country for the last time in October 2006, I knew I would have to speak and write about my experiences. I was not shy about recounting the stresses and strains of having my research permit revoked. News of my forced exit and stoppage of my research soon spread among academic and activist communities.

I had no thought at the time that my work was activist, insofar as I designed my project to situate ordinary Rwandans as people who were living their lives in a post-conflict setting.[6] As such, I understood my role to be that of a listener, to provide a space for me, as a foreigner researcher, to centre vulnerable emotions – fear, empathy, anger, despair – as normal human responses to violence (Robinson 2011). Unstable, messy, and contradictory emotions – from researched and researcher alike – must be allowed to fester and flow, for emotional response to everyday human behaviour influence not only how we listen, but also to whom we choose to listen (Shesterinina 2018), which turns the tables on the normal ethical standard of thinking through who speaks how, and to whom (Kobayashi 1994). Listening well is hard work; it requires an ethic of engagement, so we begin to hear what is not said (Fujii 2010; 2012). This matters most in settings such as post-genocide Rwanda, where listening to what is said, how it is said and the body language that accompanies speech (or silence) can be instructive of the broader social and political climate.

---

[6] My colleagues at Colgate University welcomed the possibility of activism as our pre-tenure mentoring programme as well as our tenure and promotion policies reward public scholarship. As my intellectual home is in the interdisciplinary Peace and Conflict Studies programme, I was encouraged to write op-eds and policy reports. As such, I did not experience any backlash from colleagues, and when Rwandan Twitter trolls tried to sully my professional reputation, Colgate's communications department came to my rescue. This supportive institutional environment is increasingly rare in the United States (and elsewhere), as harassment of activist academics is commonplace as Zevallos (2017) explains. See also Couture 2017 and Pulido 2008 on managing institutional challenges to scholarly activism.

A Triple 'R' Ethic

My efforts to hear ordinary Rwandans, in their own words, required more than a commitment to being fully human. A humanist approach required a clear sense of the variety of relationships I developed, relationships to which I was accountable through a triple 'R' ethic: Respect (for those on whose lives my research is based), Reciprocity (with my readers through dissemination), and Responsibility (accountability to how my research tells the story of my participants). This triple ethic developed during write up, resulting in a practice of engagement that was more concerned about ensuring that my analysis was 'true to the voices' of all who participated in my research rather than to the traditional positivist standards of what counts as social science in the Western academy (Wilson 2008, 101. Cf., Schwartz-Shea 2006; Yanow 2009).

My understanding of, and appreciation for, this triple ethic made plain to whom I was responsible, beyond the traditional audiences of other academics, and myself, as a scholar writing to generate new, or at least extend existing, academic knowledge. I was first and foremost responsible to the thirty-seven Rwandans who consented to share their testimonies with me, to document as clearly as I could, their individual and collective experience, to respect their humanity as people who have lived through mass atrocity in their own voices, whether as survivor, perpetrator, bystander, rescuer, or witness. In the process of documenting and telling their stories, I also had a duty to respect the context of their lives, to interpret their lives through the historical, political, social and economic realities that shape their present. As such, relational accountability to people extends to the ideas, concepts, theories, and methods that I chose to conduct my research. A sense of accountability to ideas means that researchers are transparent in the choices they make, when and why. I further recognise this is a tall order, especially since journal articles and other academic products, have word count limits that preclude a full exposition of the how and why of research, and the relationships that make up a body of knowledge, as a minimum standard of working 'with' rather than 'on'.

Relationship to Ideas and to People

In recognising the relationships – to people and to ideas – that frame our experience of research, we appreciate that we do not own the knowledge just because our design, method, and write up brought the information to light. Nor do we have control over how the work is received by audiences other than the intended academic ones. In my case, I included my personal experience of research in my first book, published in 2013 after I had already published a number of journal articles and book chapters. I wrote a lengthy, subjective Preface and Acknowledgements that I hoped would do two things; first, to make clear the twisting intellectual and personal path I took in deciding to work with ordinary Rwandans as part of my feminist, interpretative epistemology, and second to begin to describe in my own words how my work was stopped by the government. I thought that telling my story would end the discussion – among my academic peers and Rwandans – about what had done to raise the ire of the government and how I managed its interference in my project (Thomson 2009a; 2010; 2011; 2013b). I saw this as a minimum standard of transparency to set out the research choices I made, both consciously and those made on-the-fly, in reaction to the difficulties of having my project stopped and my passport seized.

When I defended my dissertation in 2009, I had little interest in being part of the everyday organising or protesting against the government in Kigali, even as I saw how my research was understood by many readers as critical of the RPF government. Some readers, notably some Rwandans but also a handful of colleagues, saw my work as a product of a grudge I held against the government. Others, particularly Rwandans who longed for political change, seized on my work as emblematic of the way in which Kigali deals with critics. I did not see myself as a political opponent or critic, as my writing focused on presenting my research findings, which were indeed critical of government policy, not the RPF leadership. My misstep at the time was not to appreciate the extent to which the Rwandans who used my research for their own political ends expected me to act as their advocate. I sometimes felt that they expected me to share my ideas and energy at their behest. I considered this an unreasonable expectation, leading me to feel put-upon and even resentful. In hindsight, I should have simply said that my priorities left little time for accepting every request to present my findings. I could have also been more honest when fielding requests to speak that I was busy working towards tenure (awarded in April 2017), and happily ferrying my kids to their art classes and soccer practices. However, in hindsight, I should have realised that I could not hide behind my academic identity to avoid their social justice expectations of me. As much as I was a reluctant collaborator, the fact remains that I could have better grappled with how my research would be read and interpreted by activist communities.

'Voicing the Voiceless': The Lessons of Critique

The Pain of Self-Scrutiny

The fieldwork I undertook to answer the questions I had about Rwanda since 1994 was difficult, for I was largely self-trained to do so. Beyond the informal training of the nine months it took to be granted human subjects ethics approval by my university, I had no formal ethnographic training. Only a handful of texts provided answers about the lives and life worlds of ordinary Rwandans (e.g., de Lame 2005; Newbury 1998). In many ways, I was flying by the seat of my pants, relying on a mixture of intuition and local knowledge, modifying my process as I encountered a variety of challenges to doing the research as approved by my university. I was hardly a scholar-activist, in practice or in my own understanding of the concept. In 2008, as I started to write up my research for publication in academic venues, I also began to write policy briefs and opinion-editorials. I was keen to share the voices of ordinary Rwandans with English-speaking readers living in the so-called West, to include the voices of ordinary Rwandans to illustrate the human cost for some of the RPF's post-genocide reconciliation policies. This led some Rwandans, particularly those living in Belgium and Canada, to declare me a voice for the voiceless, an honorific I barely recognised.

At the time, I had yet to realise my responsibilities to my readers, which I now understand as an ethical minimum. At the time, however, I was squarely focused on my academic career, having earned back-to-back post-doctoral fellowships, first at the University of Ottawa then at Hampshire College, before landing a tenure-track position in July 2012. My academic motivation was (and remains) bringing in the lived experiences of those subject to state power, to understand how state-led politics disrupt everyday life and endanger individual networks of support and dependence in the name of policy success.[7]

That I too was subject to the power of the Rwandan state, thus having a front-row seat to how political power operates in the lives of ordinary people, I opted to include in my Preface a personal reflection on the twists and turns that brought me to do the research that I did, and what it meant to have it stopped. In sharing how the relationships I developed with a handful of Rwandans from all walks of life, and

---

7 My current research, started in 2012, studies the self-help networks of refugee women from African countries living in Nairobi, Kenya and Cape Town, South Africa. See Thomson 2013c.

my subsequent house arrest, I realised were a product of local power relations. Given that my research was forcibly stopped, I wanted to be honest about how I approached 'the field', how I understood my positionality as a white Canadian, and to illustrate my understanding of reflexivity as a feminist mode of telling the story of how I chose my topic and understood government interference in my research project. My intent was to 'dismantle the smokescreen' of research impartiality and objectivity that filled the pages of many of the political science texts I consulted in writing my 2009 dissertation and the 2013 book on which it was based (England 1994, 81).

I could have realised that I was already walking the fine line between being a scholar and being an activist. I see now that my work was (and remains) activist in outlook and scope, something that is central to feminist scholarship (Bickham Mendez 2008, 136–38). This realisation led me to start to teach undergraduate courses on human rights advocacy and transnational activist networks, which in turn led me to read widely so I could reflect deeply on how scholars juggle the dual roles of scholar and activist. I came to embrace the label, teaching it as a series of intellectual commitments and personal characteristics, namely direct policy engagement with solving practical problems, with a view to having them put on the agendas of policymakers. All told, I learned that being an activist in sensibility and practice is a blending of political commitments with scholarly research agendas.

In hindsight, I can see why some readers viewed my Preface as framed by a series of clichés about ethnic violence in 'Africa', especially as I wrote about how witnessing an act of targeted violence in Madagascar had affected me, and in turn my research process in Rwanda (Wainaina 2006).[8] I now see that some readers saw something self-congratulatory, neo-colonial and perhaps even self-righteous in my narrative, even as this was not my intention while writing (Illich 1968). I was also honest about my post-traumatic stress diagnosis, as both a product of my personal and professional life in Africa, something which rubbed some reviewers the wrong way. I

---

[8] My purpose was to demonstrate how my work for different United Nations agencies personally affected me, and hence my research topic, methodology, and so on. Many of the twenty-four authors who reviewed my book in academic journals failed to fully appreciate my disdain for the UN, and how my work for them shaped my research question and methodology. Compare a reprimanding review by (Holmes 2014) with a substantive one (Jessee 2014), and one by a fellow political scientist (Chakravarty 2017).

can now see why I was still in those days referring to my illness as a 'disorder', not as a normal reaction to witnessing human suffering (Auchter 2019).

Voiceless by Choice?

When asked to write for this event or that public lecture organised by dissident Rwandans, I situated myself as an academic whose work theorises the power relationships that shaped the lives of rural Rwandans. I never really thought much about the perception that I was 'voicing the voiceless', as I do not think people are voiceless by choice. They are 'deliberately silenced' or 'preferably unheard'; as Arundhati Roy poignantly said in 2004. I told myself that academics, especially foreign ones, were to remain above the messiness of the politics of peoples' lives (Kapoor 2004; Spivak 1993). I considered my writing on how to ethically undertake human subjects research with vulnerable and marginal populations to be a form of 'giving back', even as I understood the ethical duty to give back to the people who participated in my research to be woefully inadequate. My responsibility was to tell the stories of rural Rwandans in as much detail as academic writing allows, going so far as to excerpt their narratives as much as I could.

While I busied myself with publishing well and often, in pursuit of an academic career, I soon spent a good portion of my evenings and weekends engaged with Rwandans in the diaspora, whether they had political aspirations or not. Many simply wanted to discuss their home country with an outsider who knew the place, to lament the political or human rights situation, or to share their hopes and dreams for Rwanda. I tried not to engage with them as activists, but rather as ordinary people who knew of how I was told to leave the country after the government stopped my research. I considered the many conversations I had with different Rwandans as an example of engaged scholarship, for I spoke up for and wrote about political issues they dare not try.

The rural Rwandans whose experiences filled the pages of my first book were not well represented in the political events organised by those in the diaspora. This troubled me. And, as an introvert who needs a lot of alone time, getting involved in Rwandan politics was not a priority, even as I was aware of the challenges Rwandans in the diaspora faced to participate in public life at home. Ultimately, being pushed to think through how to navigate my externally imposed role as a 'voice for the voiceless' made me a better social scientist. In interrogating how my research was received by Rwandan activists, I had to really think about how my research practices, my structural privileges in the academy, and my foreign positionality shape my writing. I was able to do so because I had to understand how my research, and the structures that made it possible, affected Rwandans, and not just those who participated in my research, but anyone who made use of it. In other words, this meant thinking through what it means to voice the voiceless in conversation with activist Rwandans, an audience I did not consider and should have throughout my research process, from design to dissemination.

The Politics of Voicelessness

Navigating the terrain between academic critiques of my first book and figuring out how to work with Rwandan dissidents led me to assume an activist identity. Thinking through the label and what it means to different audiences lead me to understand my own positionality as a foreign scholar and to advocate for greater reflexivity, part of which is recognising its limits and pitfalls as a form of self-scrutiny (D'Arcangelis 2017; Fujii 2016). I learned a lot that now informs my teaching and graduate student mentoring – particularly when my students are embarking on their own research projects in foreign, post-conflict environments. I now focus on guiding them to develop their own self-reflexive awareness of the ethical dimensions of research, the sources of structural and personal privilege that researchers take for granted, and a deeper sense of the power dynamics that underpin relationships in and out of 'the field'.

Being labelled a 'voice for the voiceless' taught me a lot about research as a series of relationships with people and with ideas. I recognise now that the label made me uncomfortable because I can now better see that speaking for those considered 'voiceless' shows little insight into the structural and political conditions that render large swathes of society voiceless. As such, proclaiming me a voice for the voiceless ignores the conditions for voicelessness in society, leaving those I studied to remain 'voiceless' while allowing me to take the heat in speaking what activists could not or would not say as they work to imagine and build a Rwanda where they can speak up.

Academics must realise that there is little that our work can do in places like Rwanda where voicelessness means political criticism is punished and speaking out is risky. The voices of the so-called voiceless are missing, and this is a structural reality in a society where political elites speak for, not with, rural Rwandans, both historically and today

(Newbury and Newbury 2000). In responding to calls to voice the voiceless, we researchers and writers need to practice humility, for we cannot document local realities, centring the experiences of non-elite, ordinary people without due regard for the relationships that make our research possible. As foreign researchers, we must also ask ourselves an additional question: can local researchers do the research? If they can, does our research project make it difficult for them to do their work, or does it contribute to dialogue and debate? In other words, ask yourself, does my work take up space from others doing the work? Or does your work create space for others to be heard on their own terms? Is my voice, in the form of activism, working to abolish the conditions of voicelessness in those whose lives I study?

Of course, abolishing voicelessness is a normative aspiration, but I set it out as a minimum ethic of dissemination, to provide a framework of relational accountability for researchers to think about the politics of write up and publication. As I noted above, we are accountable to those whose words and ideas form the basis of our scholarship. These relationships are the backbone of qualitative research in the social sciences, but scholars tend to overlook the messier parts of both human contradiction and contextual complexity to tell a coherent, compelling, and singular story. Relational accountability asks us to stop and think about how our work is received, and by whom, to reflect on the ethical obligations that arise in the process of dissemination. In other words, an ethical commitment to accountability begins during the design phase and continues long after one's ideas and arguments appear in print or are orally presented.

Further Reading

Chakravarty, Anuranda. 2012. '"Partially Trusting" Field Relationships: Opportunities and Constraints of Fieldwork in Rwanda's Postconflict Setting'. *Field Methods* 24, no. 3: 251–71.

Hoover Green, Amelia and Dara Kay Cohen. 2020. 'Centering Human Subjects: The Ethics of "Desk Work" on Political Violence'. *Journal of Global Security Studies.* https://doi.org/10.1093/jogss/ogaa029. Accessed 6 August 2020.

Wilson, Shawn. 2008. *Research is Ceremony: Indigenous Research Methods.* Black Point, Nova Scotia: Fernwood Publishing.

Conclusion: Theorising Self as Ethical Research Practice

Susan Thomson, An Ansoms, and Aymar Nyenyezi Bisoka

A S THE PRECEDING chapters illustrate, researchers who work and live in fragile settings are often motivated to identify the drivers of violence, to document human rights abuses, and to learn how individuals and communities recover from violence.[1] For many researchers, including those who contributed to this book, the underlying

---

[1] Each of the contributors to this volume understand violence along a continuum of harms, recognising that everyday forms of violence can provide the necessary environmental conditions for physical violence when the political context is conducive. Civil wars, for example, often have their roots in less dramatic everyday acts: exploitation, marginalisation, powerlessness, and cultural imperialism (Kalyvas 2006; Straus 2015, 273-321; Thomson 2020; Young 2004, 37-62). Indeed, social scientists have documented the ways in which repressive political regimes that rest on physical violence of torture, terror, and other human rights abuses reproduce the violence that brought them to power in the first place (Ballvé 2020; Das 2007; Desrosiers and Thomson 2011; Jones 2009; Kesselring 2017; Scheper-Hughes 2004). Even as the victors proclaim peace, everyday forms of violence persist, and are often made more pointed in society through a series of 'little' violences found in the structures, habitus, and mentalities of everyday life, of what Mbembe (1992, 22) calls 'the intimacy of tyranny'. Each of the contributors to this volume acknowledge that all societies are marked by everyday forms

rationale is to study and record the lives of people, who, historically speaking, would otherwise remain unknown, or whose stories are told by local elites or foreign humanitarians. Central to this mode of understanding violence from the perspective of those subject to it, are systematic and careful efforts to diminish the distinction between the researcher-as-authority and the informant-as-subject. This is the unifying theme of our collection. Each contributor presents a personal essay which illustrates the importance of understanding the Self as an instrument of knowledge production, and to better understand the ethic of self-knowledge. In so doing, our authors affirm something that all field-based researchers know – academic knowledge develops out of specific social and political contexts and in collaboration with a variety of actors, most notably the people who consent to take part in our research.

Indeed, as scholars know all too well, the production of knowledge obeys disciplinary standards; the primary one being that what we know is preceded by what we think – that is our implicit and explicit biases – which in turn determines our methodology and methods (Simon 1979. See also Macamo in this book). In other words, presumed *a priori* knowledge informs what is possible for us, as individuals to know, and how we think we know it determines what counts as knowledge. Context – historical, political, social, and so on – is a critical factor in challenging what we think we know, or what we think we need to know about a particular event, place, or people. As such, bringing together a diverse range of scholars from a variety of backgrounds enlivens what counts as knowledge in the confines of the Western academy, while generating new ways of thinking about what we think we know, and how through an ethic of fieldwork.

Reflexivity and Positionality in Research

We are hardly the first to centre the Self as an instrument of knowledge. Indeed, anthropologists, oral historians, philosophers, and sociologists have long done so, in myriad locations and among those who study the politics of the 'everyday'[2] and the politics of emotions in a given context

---

of violence. What differs is how violence is made real in people's lives, and how everyday violence is sanctioned or legitimated by the state.

[2]   The concept of 'the everyday' allows analysts to identify and theorise the unwritten and informal rules of everyday life. For a summary of the concept as employed by social theorists, see Kalekin-Fishman (2013).

(e.g, Blee 1993; Fraser 1979; Fujii 2010; Jessee 2017; Kobayashi 1994; Morgan 1983; Sayigh 1998; Thomson 2010; White 2000). However, in this book, our focus provides an introspective perspective – of the private thoughts and personal choices – that researchers make during and after fieldwork, something anthropologists also consider but rarely in violence-affected locales (but see McLean and Leibing 2007; Robben and Sluka 2012). As such, this book addresses two key principles of ethical fieldwork, regardless of field site, disciplinary training, or the intersecting identities of the researcher: reflexivity and positionality. Underpinning each chapter are interlinking questions of how best to do fieldwork with how to evaluate what our participants and others tell us. To do so, each author in this book merged methodology with epistemology as a central component of analysing and critiquing the twin concepts of reflexivity and positionality in studying lives lived in violence, learning from other researchers and our own experiences (e.g., Akello 2012; Berger 2015; Bouka 2015; Fujii 2016; Madlingozi 2010; Owor Ogora 2013; Probst 2015; Wood 2006).

Our book focuses on reflexivity and positionality as a minimum standard of ethical practice for researchers, regardless of field site. Feminists have long considered the influence and effect of reflexivity and positionality as central to an ethical practice that is sensitive to power relations in qualitative research (e.g., Jagger 2014). Our book extends this intellectual tradition in conflict- and violence-affected settings in different African contexts. Indeed, anyone who carefully reads the bibliographies of each chapter in this book will be rewarded with knowledge of a broad range of decolonial, feminist, and interpretative scholarship on methods and methodology. Our authors thus explain who they are, and how their person informs how they see, smell and feel their research terrain. Each author displays an embodied sense of wonder and curiosity that drives their research, a method to be embraced for its ability to capitalise on the inevitable surprises and disruptions that are the hallmark of research (Janesick 2003; Lobo-Guerrero 2013, 28).

We explicitly call for greater reflexivity as a way to manage the inevitable range of emotions that accompany fieldwork, and to harness the interpretative and analytical value of a range of emotions in and beyond the field. Our authors deploy reflexivity as an interpretative device that includes not only how to theorise about the role of the Self in all stages of the research process, but also how to assess the social and political context from which their identity is derived, notably class, gender, and race. An examination of one's positionality is central to the process of knowledge production, as personal values, world views, and structural locations in a given social, historical, and political context influence how one understands the world in which we live and work. In adopting a reflexivity-positionality approach, our authors do more than engage in a sustained process of self-evaluation that Berger (2015, 200) calls 'the process of continued internal dialogue.' Taken together, our authors illustrate the importance of theorising informal observations in the field (Djelloul; Nyenyezi Bisoka; Vlavanou; and Vuninga) and heightening the researcher's ethical awareness of working relationships forged in the research process (Ansoms; Mudinga; and Thomson).

By offering their reflections on the reflexivity-positionality dialectic, our authors collectively analyse the importance of a sustained engagement with the ethical elements of fieldwork. Moreover, our authors show that foregrounding the power imbalances that mark various relationships of academic work – from representatives of ethics review boards and dissertation supervisors, to local actors as well as peer reviewers and readers – can contribute to the integrity and rigour of the research project. By becoming aware of and theorising the Self, researchers 'can turn unplanned, unscripted, and unstructured observations [...] into valuable sources of data and insight (Fujii 2014, 1150; Manning 2018). In other words, context matters as it determines how the researcher relates to people and place, as well as time and space. Understanding and explaining sociopolitical and historical context is as much about embodied reactions as it is about material and analytical ones.

Each of our contributing authors are committed to work closely with local actors, to reflect on their presence in the lives of people they know, whether personally or professionally, to assess how these relationships are at the heart of the how they know what they know, and to recognise the challenges of separating one's private life from their professional lives. To illustrate our point, we as editors compiled a diverse range of scholars, at different stages of their academic lives, and based in multiple locations in Africa, Europe, and North America.

Implicit in each chapter is the fundamental belief that the first duty of scholars is the ethical treatment of the people affected by our research. This extends to those who consent to participate in our interviews and focus groups. It also includes community members, assistants, translators, and others 'in the field' as well as peer reviewers, colleagues, students, and other end-users, including members of diasporic communities and simply interested members of the general public, whether at home or abroad.

Of particular merit is the contribution of Africa-born researchers working in African-locations, many of whom conduct research in their countries of origin. The intellectual perspectives and emotional issues that they bring to research are rare in the academy, as their expertise is often mined without attribution or, depending on the type of publication, in a footnote as an assistant, fixer, or translator. By bringing together this collection of scholars from the continent, our book offers novel ways to think about reflexivity and positionality in their own words and through their own epistemological lens. The ethical, emotional, and practical realities of being an 'inside-insider' make fieldwork all the more challenging, thus providing important lessons and advice for qualitative researchers, as their nuanced under-standing of research at or with 'home' provides valuable guidance to anyone thinking of fieldwork.

Emotions are central to an ethical research practice, since to grapple with emotion is foremost to negotiate and make sense of the rela-tionships that define the fieldwork enterprise (see Foreword). Each chapter in our book foregrounds the emotions of the researcher, the researched, and the many on-the-ground collaborators; our book lays bare the process of grappling with one's emotions, and how feelings inform and shape our process of data collection, interpretation, write-up, and dissemination. Said otherwise, the ways in which researchers understand the range of emotions that they experience in the field and during the reflective stage of writing up is a form of critical epistemo-logical self-observation. As such, our authors embrace an interpretivist dialectic in which feelings inform their analysis and their analyses give meaning to how they make sense of the people they study. The result is a collection of chapters that reveal the ambiguities and inconsistencies that emerge at all stages of fieldwork. In eschewing the traditional dis-ciplinary boundaries, our authors reveal the value of honestly reflecting on how their positionality shapes the 'what' and 'how' of researching lives lived in, and affected by, violence.

Epistemology, Methodology, and Method

In eschewing a narrowly technical discussion of methodology in favour of an explicit reflexivity-positionality hermeneutic, our analysis cri-tiques and ultimately rejects a positivist perspective. All the same, we remain mindful that the institutional ethics review boards, particu-larly in the United States, South Africa, and Canada, operate within a positivist frame that positions the researcher as an objective observer whose task it is to report in a value-free way what they found in the field. While we agree on the minimal ethical standard of 'do no harm,'[3] we also question the approach of ethics as a matter of morality aligned to universally defined values of how to act ethically. The result is a checklist of how to meet ethical standards (of consent, anonymity, confidentiality, and so on), rather than a process designed to develop an embodied ethical sensibility. Research ethics are an on-going responsibility, not a discrete task (Fujii 2012; Thaler 2019). For example, scholars based at American universities, or those outside the US who find themselves subject to American ethics protocols through collaboration, have rightfully argued against the ethical imperialism of the American system (e.g., Schrag 2006, 2010; Yanow and Schwartz-Shea 2008) while pushing back on its positivist protocols (Thomson 2013b; Yanow and Schwartz-Shea 2016).

To challenge the weight of the positivist paradigm on research with human subjects, particularly in the social sciences, we take inspiration from the work of Sandra Harding (1987) to distinguish between the three elements embedded in how we do research: epistemology, methodology, and method. An epistemology is a theory about knowledge, specifically who can know what and under what circumstances valid knowledge can be produced. A method is a technique for gathering and analysing information that becomes data through interpretation. Information is gathered by listening, watching, and studying documents and other materials (film, newspapers, websites, and so on). Researchers then organise data through the conceptual frameworks we, as individuals, bring to the information, and by looking for patterns or themes. The choices that researchers make of how to use these methods (interviews, focus groups, archives, etc) are one's methodology. Each methodology is based on often unexamined (but

---

3   For example, the Belmont Report holds that the foremost ethical obligation of researchers, and thus their very first duty is to the ethical treatment of human subjects (US Department of Health and Human Services 1979). The report follows from decades of unethical treatment in various experiments with human subjects, including the revelation of Nazi experimentation after the Second World War, the Milgram experiment at Yale University, and the Tuskegee experiments, in which hundreds of black men of African descent were injected with syphilis. For analysis of these experiments, and their role in creating the current ethics framework and resulting protocols, see Jones (1993); Schrag (2010).

sometimes explicit) assumptions about what knowledge is and how knowing is best accomplished (Ladson-Billings 2003; Leonardo 2018).

By decoupling the elision of method and epistemology, methodology emerges as a site to work out how we can do what we do. Part of this decoupling is making space for self-dialogue about reflexivity and positionality. Thinking deeply and in a sustained way about the role of the Self in all phases of the research process allows us to ask questions that mediate the reflexivity-positionality framework we employ. These questions include: is the way we gather and interpret data consistent with how we think knowledge should be created or disseminated (Ansoms)? Is this process in line with how our participants think knowledge should be created (Djelloul, Vuninga)? To whom do we owe an answer (Mudinga, Thomson)? What kind of assumptions underlie how we approach the field, the questions we ask, the relationships we make, how we listen to and engage with research participants and others (Ansoms, Vlavonou)? Finally, is the way in which we interpret our data to make claims about how things are, consistent with what actually happened (Nyenyezi Bisoka)? This handful of questions that the researcher could ask themselves puts the technical details of method and methodology into social and political context that in turn provides an avenue for analysis of the role of researcher emotion, and the consequence of emotionality, squarely in the realm of how we know what we know.

As our authors collectively demonstrate, their individual confrontation with the subjective element of a range of emotions – pain, fear, hope, empathy, and more – provides an avenue for critical reflexivity as a method (Deleuze 1986; Foucault 1980). As such, we view the personal insights of our authors as an academically subversive exercise. By foregrounding their multiple and varied ways of reflecting on their work as researchers and their human responses to their work, each essay in our collection demonstrates how reflexivity and positionality are part and parcel of the process of knowledge production.

Taken together, our collection provides a bridge for researchers who want to work through the emotional complexities of working in conflict-affected or violent settings. Our aim is to normalise researcher emotions, both here and there, so as to provide space for scholars, doctoral students, dissertation advisors, and others involved in the academic enterprise, to consider the human effects and costs of research and to acknowledge and tackle the vulnerabilities that emerge at all stages of fieldwork.

Bibliography

Abrahamsen, Rita. 2003. 'African Studies and the Postcolonial Challenge'. *African Affairs* 102, no. 407: 189–210.

Abu-Lughod, Lila. 1988. 'Dutiful Daughter'. In *Arab Women in the Field: Studying Your Own Society*, edited by Soraya Altorki and Camillia Fawzi El-Solh, 139–62. Syracuse: Syracuse University Press.

Abu-Lughod, Lila. 1996. 'Writing Against Culture'. In *Recapturing Anthropology: Working in the Present*, edited by Richard G. Fox, 137–62. Sante Fe: School of American Research Press.

Adamson, Fiona B. 2006. 'Crossing Borders: International Migration and National Security'. *International Security* 31, no. 1: 165–99.

Adenaike, Carolyn Keyes. 1996. 'Life During Research'. In *In Pursuit of History: Fieldwork in Africa*, edited by Carolyn Keyes Adenaike and Jan Vansina, 1–10. Portsmouth: Heinemann.

Agier, Michel. 2016. 'Epistemological decentring: At the root of a contemporary and situational anthropology'. *Anthropological Theory* 1, no. 16: 22–47.

Akello, Grace. 2012. 'The importance of the autobiographic self during research among wartime children in northern Uganda'. *Medische Antropologie* 24, no. 2: 289–300.

Altorki, Soraya. 1988. 'At Home in the Field'. In *Arab Women in the Field: Studying Your Own Society*, edited by Soraya Altorki and Camillia Fawzi El-Solh, 49–68. Syracuse: Syracuse University Press.

Altorki, Soraya and Camillia Fawzi El-Solh, eds. 1988. *Arab Women in the Field: Studying Your Own Society*. Syracuse: Syracuse University Press.

Ansoms, An. 2012. 'The Story behind the Findings: Ethical and Emotional Challenges of Field Research in Conflict-Prone Environments'. Working Paper Series, *Conflict in Difficult Settings*. http://conflictfieldresearch. colgate.edu/wp-content/uploads/2015/02/Ethical_Emotional_Challenges.pdf. Accessed 9 July 2019.

Ansoms, An. 2013. 'Dislodging Power Structures in Rural Rwanda: From "Disaster Tourist" to "Transfer Gate."' In *Emotional and Ethical Challenges for Field Research in Africa,* edited by Susan Thomson, An Ansoms, and Jude Murison, 42–56. London: Palgrave MacMillan.

Ansoms, An and Aymar Nyenyezi Bisoka. 2016. 'Théâtre-action en Afrique: une Utopie de la recherche de terrain.' *Revue Nouvelle* 71, no. 5: 16–31.

Atkinson, Paul. 2009. 'Ethics and Ethnography.' *Twenty-First Century Society* 4, no. 1: 17–30.

Auchter, Jessica. 2019. 'Narrating Trauma: Individuals, Communities, Storytelling.' *Millennium: Journal of International Studies* 47, no. 2: 272–83.

Ballvé, Teo. 2020. 'Investigative Ethnography: A Spatial Approach to Economies of Violence.' *Geographical Review* 110, no. 1–2: 238–51.

Bank, Andrew and Leslie J. Bank, eds. 2013. *Inside African Anthropology: Monica Wilson and her Interpreters.* Cambridge: Cambridge University Press.

Beaud, Stéphane and Florence Weber. 2003. *Guide de l'enquête de Terrain: produire et analyser les données ethnographiques.* Paris: La Découverte.

Beecher, Henry K. 1966. 'Ethics and Clinical Research.' *Bulletin of the World Health Organization: the International Journal of Public Health* 79, no. 4: 367–72.

Berger, Roni. 2015. 'Now I See It, Now I Don't: Researcher's Position and Reflexivity in Qualitative Research.' *Qualitative Research* 15, no. 2: 219–34.

Berlant, Lauren. 1997. 'Feminism and the Institutions of Intimacy.' In *The Politics of Research,* edited by E. Ann Kaplan and George Levine, 143–61. New Brunswick: Rutgers University Press.

Berry, Maya J., Claudia Chávez Argüelles, Shanya Cordis, Sarah Ihmoud, and Elizabeth Velásquez Estrada. 2017. 'Toward a Fugitive Anthropology: Gender, Race, and Violence in the Field.' *Cultural Anthropology* 32, no. 4: 537–65.

Bhattacharya, Srobana. 2014. 'Institutional Review Board and International Field Research in Conflict Zones.' *PS: Political Science & Politics* 47, no. 4: 840–44.

Bickham Mendez, Jennifer. 2008. 'Globalizing Scholar Activism: Opportunities and Dilemmas through a Feminist Lens.' In *Theory, Politics, and Methods of Activist Scholarship,* edited by Charles R. Hale, 136–63. Berkeley: University of California Press.

Bilge, Sirma. 2009. 'Théorisations Féministes de l'Intersectionnalité.' *Diogène* 1, no. 225: 70–88.

Blee, Kathleen M. 1993. 'Evidence, Empathy, and Ethics: Lessons from Oral Histories of the Klan'. *The Journal of American History* 80, no. 2: 596–606

Blomley, Nicholas K. 1994. 'Activism and the Academy'. *Environment and Planning: Society and Space* 13: 235–37.

Bodson, Daniel. 2000. *Les Villageois*. Louvain: L'Harmattan.

Borgatti, Stephane P. and Daniel S. Halgin. 2011. 'On Network Theory'. *Organization Science* 22, no. 5: 1168–81.

Bouka, Yolande. 2015 'Researching Violence in Africa as a Black Woman: Notes from Rwanda'. Working Paper Series, *Conflict in Difficult Settings*. http://conflictfieldresearch.colgate.edu/wp-content/uploads/2015/05/Bouka_WorkingPaper-May2015.pdf. Accessed 9 March 2020.

Bourdieu, Pierre and Loic J.D. Wacquant. 1992. *An Invitation to Reflexive Sociology*. Chicago: University of Chicago Press.

Bourdieu, Pierre, Jean-Claude Chamboredon, and Jean-Claude Passeron. 1983. *Le Métier de Sociologue*. Paris: Mouton.

Boumaza, Magali, and Aurélie Campana. 2007. 'Enquêter en Milieu "Difficile"'. *Revue Française de Science Politique* 57, no. 1: 5–25.

Bourke, Joanna. 2006. *Fear: A Cultural History*. Berkeley: Counterpoint Press.

Bozzoli, Belinda. 1985. 'Migrant Women and South African Social Change: Biographical Approaches to Social Analysis'. *African Studies* 44, no 1: 87–96.

Bozzoli, Belinda and Mmantho Nkotsoe. 1991. *Women of Phokeng: Consciousness Life Strategy and Migrancy in South Africa, 1900–1983*. London: Heinemann.

Brewis, Joanna. 2014. 'The Ethics of Researching Friends: On Convenience Sampling in Qualitative Management and Organization Studies'. *British Journal of Management* 25, no. 4: 849–62.

Brooks, Abigail, and Sharlene Nagy Hesse-Biber. 2007. 'An Invitation to Feminist Research'. In *Feminist Research Practice*, edited by Sharlene Nagy Hesse-Biber and Patricia Lina Leavy, 1–25. London: Sage.

Brown, Brené. 2013. 'Brené Brown on Empathy'. YouTube video. 2m53s. Posted by "The RSA." December 10. https://youtu.be/1Evwgu369Jw. Accessed 27 April 2018.

Brown, Stephen. 2009. 'Dilemma of Self-Representation and Conduct in the Field'. In *Surviving Field Research: Working in Violent and Difficult Situations*, edited by Chandra Lekha Sriram, John C. King, Julie Mertus, Olga Martín-Ortega, and Joanna Herman, 213–26. London: Routledge.

Buckley-Zistel, Susanne. 2007. 'Ethnographic Research after Violent Conflicts: Personal Reflections on Dilemmas and Challenges'. *Journal of Peace, Development and Security* 10: 1–9.

Butz, David, and Kathryn Besio. 2009. 'Autoethnography'. *Geography Compass* 3, no. 5: 1660–74.

Calhoun, Craig. 2008. 'Forward'. In *Engaging Contradictions: Theory, Politics, and Methods of Activist Scholarship*, edited by Charles R. Hale, xii–xxvi. Berkeley: University of California Press.

Campbell, Susanna P. 2017. 'Ethics of Research in Conflict Environments'. *Journal of Global Security Studies* 2, no. 1: 89–101.

Campigotto, Marie, Rachel Dobbels, and Elsa Mescoli. 2017. 'La Pratique du Terrain "Chez Soi" Entre Familiarité, Altérité et Engagement'. *Emulations* 22: 7–15.

Caponio, Tiziana. 2005. 'Policy Networks and Immigrants' Associations in Italy: The Cases of Milan, Bologna and Naples'. *Journal of Ethnic and Migration Studies* 31, no 5: 931–50.

Carlier, Omar. 1995. *Entre Nation et Jihad. Histoire des Radicalismes Algériens.* Paris: Presses de Sciences Po.

Carpenter, Charli. 2012. '"You Talk of Terrible Things so Matter-of-Factly in this Language of Science": Constructing Human Rights in the Academy'. *Perspectives on Politics* 10, no. 2: 363–83.

Carter, Sean. 2005. 'The Geopolitics of Diaspora'. *Area* 37, no.1: 154–63.

Chacko, Elizabeth. 2004. 'Positionality and Praxis: Fieldwork Experiences in Rural India'. *Singapore Journal of Tropical Geography* 25, no. 1: 51–63.

Chakravarty, Anuranda. 2012. '"Partially Trusting" Field Relationships: Opportunities and Constraints of Fieldwork in Rwanda's Postconflict Setting'. *Field Methods* 24, no. 3: 251–71.

Chakravarty, Anuranda. 2017. 'Review of *Whispering Truth to Power: Everyday Day Resistance to Reconciliation in Postgenocide Rwanda*'. *Perspective on Politics* 15, no. 4: 1189–90.

Chatzifotiou, Sevaste. 2000. 'Conducting Qualitative Research on Wife Abuse: Dealing with the Issue of Anxiety'. *Sociological Research Online* 5, no. 2: 1–10.

Chowdhury, Rashedur. 2017. 'Rana Plaza Fieldwork and Academic Anxiety: Some Reflections'. *Journal of Management Studies* 54, no. 7: 1111–17.

Clark-Kazak, Christina R. 2012. 'Research as "Social Work" in Kampala? Managing Expectations, Compensation and Relationships in Research with Unassisted Urban Refugees from the Democratic Republic of Congo'. In *Emotional and Ethical Challenges for Field Research in Africa*, edited by Susan Thomson, An Ansoms, and Jude Murison, 96–106. London: Palgrave MacMillan.

Coetzee, Carli. 2019. *Written Under the Skin: Blood and Intergenerational Memory in South Africa.* London: James Currey.

Cohn, Carol. 1987. 'Sex and Death in the Rational World of Defense Intellectuals.' *Signs* 12, no. 4: 687–718.

Compaoré, W. R. Nadège. 2017. 'Voici la Jeune Femme qui Veut Poser des Questions : Composer avec le Genre et une Positionnalité Changeante durant l'enquête de Terrain.' *Études Internationales* 48, no. 1: 105–16.

Couture, Stéphane. 2017. 'Commentary. Activist–Scholarship: The Complicated Entanglements of Activism and Research Work.' *Canadian Journal of Communication* 42: 143–47.

Cramer, Christopher, Laura Hammond, and Johan Potters, eds. 2011. *Researching Violence in Africa: Ethical and Methodological Challenges.* Leiden: Brill.

Cronin-Furman, Kate and Milli Lake. 2018. 'Ethics Abroad: Fieldwork in Fragile and Violent Contexts.' *PS: Political Science and Politics* 51, no. 3: 607–14.

D'Arcangelis, Carol Lynne. 2017. 'Revelations of a White Settler Woman Scholar-Activist: The Fraught Promise of Self-Reflexivity.' *Cultural Studies <–> Critical Methodologies* 18, no.: 5: 339–53.

Darling, Jonathon. 2014. 'Emotions, Encounters and Expectations: The Uncertain Ethics of "The Field".' *Journal of Human Rights Practice* 6, no. 2: 201–12.

Das, Veena. 2007. *Life and Words: Violence and the Descent into the Ordinary.* Berkeley: University of California Press.

Davidson, Judy. 2004. 'Dilemmas in Research: Issues of Vulnerability and Disempowerment for the Social Worker/Researcher.' *Journal of Social Work Practice* 18, no. 3: 379–93.

Davis, Christine S. and Deborah C. Breede. 2015. 'Holistic Ethnography: Emotion, Contemplation and Dialogue in Ethnographic Fieldwork.' *The Journal of Contemplative Inquiry* 2, no. 1: 77–100.

De Gasquet, Béatrice. 2015. 'Que fait le Féminisme au Regard de l'Ethnographe?' *SociologieS.* 26 May.

de Lame, Danielle. 2005. *A Hill among a Thousand: Transformations and Ruptures in Rural Rwanda*, translated by Helen Arnold. Madison: University of Wisconsin Press.

de Sardan, Jean-Pierre Olivier. 2015. *Epistemology, Fieldwork and Anthropology.* London: Palgrave MacMillan.

Des Forges, Alison. 1999. *Leave None to Tell the Story: Genocide in Rwanda.* New York: Human Rights Watch.

Deleuze, Gilles. 1986. *Foucault.* Paris: Éditions de Minuit.

Delphy, Christine. 2009. *L'ennemi principal*, Tome 2. Paris: Syllepse.

Demart, Sarah. 2013. 'Congolese Migration to Belgium and Postcolonial Perspectives'. *African Diaspora* 6, no. 1: 1–20.

Denzin, Norman K. 2009. *The Research Act: A Theoretical Introduction to Sociological Methods.* London: Aldine Transaction Publishing.

Depelchin, Jacques. 2005. *Silences in African History: Between the Syndromes of Discovery and Abolition.* Dar-es-Salaam: Mkuki Na Nyota Publishers.

Dery, Issac. 2020. 'Negotiating positionality, reflexivity and power relations in research on men and masculinities in Ghana'. *Gender, Place & Culture: A Journal of Feminist Geography.* 27, no. 12: 1766–84.

Desrosiers, Marie-Eve and Susan Thomson. 2011. 'Rhetorical Legacies of Leadership: Projections of "Benevolent Leadership" in Pre- and Post-Genocide Rwanda'. *Journal of Modern African Studies* 49, no. 3: 431–55.

Djelloul, Ghaliya. 2017. 'Donner Corps à la Non-Violence dans les Espaces Extra-Domestiques ou Comment Incarner une Vie Digne d'être Vécue?' In *Du Genre à la Non-Violence,* edited by Cécile Defaut, 84–98. Nantes.

Djelloul, Ghaliya 2018a. 'Le Féminisme Islamique au Prisme de la Décolonialité: Dépasser l'horizon Postcolonial pour Envisager un Féminisme Pluriversel?'. *La Revue Nouvelle.* https://www.revuenouvelle.be/Le-feminisme-islamique-au-prisme-de-la. Accessed 7 September 2018.

Djelloul, Ghaliya. 2018b. 'Entre Enserrement et Desserrement, la Mobilité Spatiale des Femmes en Périphérie d'Alger'. *Métropolitiques.* Avril.

Duschesne, Sophie and Florence Haegel. 2008. *L'enquête et ses méthodes, l'entretien collectif.* Paris: Armand Colin.

Eisenhardt, Kathleen M. and Claudia Bird Schoonhoven. 1996. 'Resource-Based View of Strategic Alliance Formation: Strategic and Social Effects in Entrepreneurial Firms'. *Organization Science* 7, no. 2: 136–50.

England, Kim V.L. 1994. 'Getting Personal: Reflexivity, Positionality, and Feminist Research'. *Professional Geographer* 46, no. 1: 80–9.

Faës, Hubert. 2014. 'Sens et Valeur du Contexte en Éthique'. *Revue d'Éthique et de Théologie Morale* 3, no. 280: 11–33.

Fanon, Frantz. 1959. 'Médecine et colonialisme'. In *L'an V de la révolution algérienne.* Paris, 107–35. Paris: La Découverte.

Foucault, Michel. 1975. *Surveiller et Punir, Naissance de la Prison.* Paris: Gallimard.

Foucault, Michel. 1980. *Power/Knowledge. Selected Interviews and Writings, 1972–1977.* New York: Pantheon Books.

Foucault, Michel. 2001. *Dits et Écrits,* 2 volumes. Paris: Gallimard, Collection Quarto.

Fraser, Ronald. 1979. *Blood of Spain: An Oral History of the Spanish Civil War*. New York: Pantheon Books.

Fujii, Lee Ann. 2009. *Killing Neighbors: Webs of Violence in Rwanda*. Ithaca: Cornell University Press.

Fujii, Lee Ann. 2010. 'Shades of Truth and Lies: Interpreting Testimonies of War and Violence.' *Journal of Peace Research* 47, no. 2: 231–41.

Fujii, Lee Ann. 2012. 'Research Ethics 101: Dilemmas and Responsibilities.' *PS: Political Science and Politics* 45, no. 4: 717–23

Fujii, Lee Ann. 2014. 'Five Stories of Accidental Ethnography: Turning Unplanned Moments in the Field into Data.' *Qualitative Research* 15, no. 4: 525–39.

Fujii, Lee Ann. 2016. 'Review Essay: Politics of the "Field".' *Perspectives on Politics* 14, no. 4: 1147–52.

Gair, Susan. 2012. 'Feeling their Stories: Contemplating Empathy, Insider/Outsider Positionings, and Enriching Qualitative Research.' *Qualitative Health Research* 22, no. 1: 134–43.

Gallaher, Carolyn. 2009. 'Researching Repellent Groups: Some Methodological Considerations on how to Represent Militants, Radicals, and Other Belligerents.' In *Surviving Field Research Working in Violent and Difficult Situations*, edited by Chandra Lekha Sriram, John C. King, Julie A. Mertus, Olga Martin-Ortega, and Johanna Herman, 127–46. London: Routledge.

Garbin, David, and Marie Godin. 2013. '"Saving the Congo": Transnational Social Fields and Politics of Home in the Congolese Diaspora.' *African and Black Diaspora: An International Journal* 6, no. 2: 113–30.

Gaudet, Stéphanie, and Dominique Robert. 2018. *A Journey Through Qualitative Research: From Design to Reporting*. London: Sage.

Gauntlett, David. 2011. *Making is Connecting: The Social Meaning of Creativity, from DIY and Knitting to YouTube and web 2.0*. Cambridge: Polity Press.

Genard, Jean-Louis, and Marta Roca i Escoda. 2014. 'Les Dispositions Éthiques dans la Conduite de l'Enquête et la Livraison Publique de ses Résultats.' *SociologieS*. 24 June.

Gerbaudo, Paolo. 2018. *Tweets and the Streets: Social Media and Contemporary Activism*. London: Pluto Press.

Githaiga, Nyambura. 2016. *Building Peace That Lasts: A Study of State-Led Peacebuilding in Kenya*. Unpublished PhD dissertation, Political Studies. University of Ottawa, Canada.

Gluck, Sherna Berger, and Daphne Patai. 2016. *Women's Words: The Feminist Practice of Oral History*. London: Routledge.

Goffman, Erving. 1983. 'The Interaction Order: American Sociological Association, 1982 Presidential Address'. *American Sociological Review* 48, no. 1: 1–17.

Goffman, Erving, and Claude Zaidman. 2002. *L'Arrangement des Sexes*, translated by Hervé Maury. Paris: La Dispute.

Gold, Raymond L. 1958. 'Roles in Sociological Field Observations'. *Social Forces* 36, no. 3: 217–33.

Goodhand, Jonathan. 2000. 'Research in Conflict Zones: Ethics and Accountability'. *Forced Migration Review* 8, no. 4: 12–6.

Granovetter, Mark, 1985. 'Economic Action and Social Structure. The Problem of Embeddedness'. *American Journal of Sociology* 91, no. 3: 481–510.

Grawitz, Madeleine. 2000. *Méthodes des sciences sociales*. 11th edition. Paris: Daloz.

Green, Linda. 2005. 'Living in a State of Fear'. In *Fieldwork Under Fire: Contemporary Studies of Violence and Culture*, edited by Carolyn Nordstrom and Antonius C.G.M. Robben, 105–27. Berkeley, CA: University of California Press.

Gregory, Eve, and Mahera Ruby. 2011. '"The 'Insider/Outsider" Dilemma of Ethnography: Working with Young Children and their Families in Cross-Cultural Contexts'. *Journal of Early Childhood Research* 9, no. 2: 162–74.

Grimm, Jannis, Kevin Koehler, Ellen Lust, Ilyas Saliba and Isabell Schierenbeck. 2019. *Safer Field Research in the Social Sciences: A Guide to Human and Digital Security in Hostile Environments*. London: Sage Publishers.

Halbwachs, Maurice. 1997 [1950]. *La mémoire collective*. Paris: Albin Michel.

Hale, Charles R. 2008. 'Introduction'. In *Engaging Contradictions: Theory, Politics, and Methods of Activist Scholarship*, edited by Charles R. Hale, 1–28. Berkeley: University of California Press.

Hall, Stuart. 1996. 'New Ethnicities'. In *Stuart Hall: Critical Dialogues in Cultural Studies*, edited by Kuan-Hsing Chen, Stuart Hall, and Dave Morley, 441–49. London: Routledge.

Hammersley, Martyn. 2006. 'Ethnography: Problems and Prospects'. *Ethnography and Education* 1, no. 1: 3–14.

Harding, Sandra. 1987. 'The Method Question'. *Hypatia: A Journal of Feminist Philosophy* 2, no. 3, part 1: 19–35.

Harding, Sandra. 1991. *Whose Science? Whose Knowledge? Thinking from Women's Lives*. Ithaca: Cornell University Press.

Harding, Sandra. 1992. 'Rethinking Standpoint Epistemology: What is "Strong Objectivity?"'. *The Centennial Review* 36, no. 3: 437–70.

Hays-Mitchell, Maureen. 2001. 'Danger, Fulfilment, and Responsibility in a Violence-Plagued Society'. *Geographical Review* 91, no. ½: 311–21.

Hemming, Judy. 2009. 'Exceeding Scholarly Responsibility: IRBs and Political Constraints'. In *Surviving Field Research Working in Violent and Difficult Situations,* edited by Chandra Lekha Sriram, John C. King, Julie A. Mertus, Olga Martin-Ortega, and Johanna Herman, 21–37. London: Routledge.

Hesse-Biber, Sharlene N. 2014. 'A Re-Invitation to Feminist Research'. In *Feminist Research Practice: A Primer,* 2nd edition, edited by Sharlene N. Hesse-Biber, 1–13. Los Angeles: Sage Publications.

Hill Collins, Patricia. 1986. 'Learning from the Outsider Within: The Sociological Significance of Black Feminist Thought'. *Social Problems* 33, no. 6: 14–32.

Hill Collins, Patricia. 2013. *On Intellectual Activism.* Philadelphia: Temple University Press.

Holmes, Georgina. 2014. 'Review of *Whispering Truth to Power: Everyday Day Resistance to Reconciliation in Postgenocide Rwanda*'. *Journal of Modern African Studies* 53, no. 4: 684–86.

Hutchinson, Sharon E. 2011. 'Uncertain Ethics: Researching Civil War in Sudan'. In *Researching Violence in Africa: Ethical and Methodological Challenges,* edited by Christopher Cramer, Laura Hammond, and Johan Pottier, 79–93. Leiden: Brill.

Illich, Ivan. 1968. *To Hell with Good Intentions.* Center for Civic Reflection. http://civicreflection.org/resources/library/browse/to-hell-with-good-intentions. Accessed 21 February 2018.

Inaka, Saint José. 2016. 'Combattants and Anti-Combattants (Collabos): Congolese Transnational Politics in Pretoria'. *Strategic Review for Southern Africa* 38, no. 1: 5–28.

Jackson, Stephen. 2001. '"Nos Richesses sont Pillées!" Économies de Guerre et Rumeurs de Crime au Kivu', translated by Claire Médard. *Politique Africaine* 4: 117–35.

Jagger, Alison M., ed. 2014. *Just Methods: An Interdisciplinary Feminist Reader.* Boulder and London: Paradigm Publishers.

Janesick, Valerie J. 2003. 'The Choreography of Qualitative Research Design: Minuets, Improvisations, and Crystallization'. In *Strategies of Qualitative Inquiry,* 2nd edition, edited by Norman K. Denzin and Yvonne S. Lincoln, 46–79. Thousand Oaks: Sage Publications.

Jaquet, Chantal. 2014. *Les transclasses ou la non-reproduction.* Paris: Presses universitaires de France.

Jenkins, Sarah-Ann. 2012. *Understanding Ethnic Violence: The 2007–2008 Post-Election Crisis in Kenya.* Unpublished PhD dissertation. Aberystwyth University, Wales.

Jessee, Erin. 2014. 'Review of *Whispering Truth to Power: Everyday Day Resistance to Reconciliation in Postgenocide Rwanda'. African Conflict and Peacebuilding Review* 4, no. 2: 163–66.

Jessee, Erin. 2017. 'Managing Danger in Oral Historical Fieldwork'. *The Oral History Review* 44, no. 2: 322–47.

Jethro, Duane. 2020. *Heritage Formation and the Senses in Post-Apartheid South Africa: Aesthetics of Power.* London: Bloomsbury Academic.

Jipson, Arthur and Chad Litton. 2000. 'Body, Career and Community: The Implications of Researching Dangerous Groups'. In *Danger in the Field: Risk and Ethics in Social Research,* edited by Geraldine Lee Treweek and Stephanie Linkogle, 147–67. London: Routledge.

Johnston, Barbara Rose. 2010. 'Social Responsibility and the Anthropological Citizen'. *Current Anthropology* 51, supp. 2: S235–S247.

Jok, Madut. 2013. 'Power Dynamics and the Politics of Fieldwork under Sudan's Prolonged Conflicts'. In *Research Methods in Conflict Settings: A View from Below,* edited by Dyan Mazurana, Karen Jacobsen, and Lacey Andrews Gale, 149–67. Cambridge: Cambridge University Press.

Jones, Adam. 2009. '"When the rabbit's got the gun": Subaltern Genocide and the Genocidal Continuum'. In *Genocides by the Oppressed: Subaltern Genocide in Theory and Practice,* edited by Nicholas A. Robins and Adam Jones, 185–207. Bloomington: Indiana University Press.

Jones, James H. 1993. *Bad Blood: The Tuskegee Syphilis Experiment.* New York: The Free Press.

Jorgenson, Danny L. 1989. 'The Methodology of Participant Observation'. In *The Methodology of Participant Observation,* edited by Danny L. Jorgenson, 12–26. Thousand Oaks, CA: Sage Publications.

Joseph, Suad. 1988. 'Feminization, Familism, Self, and Politics' In *Arab Women in the Field: Studying Your Own Society,* edited by Soraya Altorki and Camillia Fawzi El-Solh, 25–48. Syracuse: Syracuse University Press.

Jourdan, Luca. 2013. 'From Humanitarian to Anthropologist: Writing at the Margins of Ethnographic Research in the Democratic Republic of Congo'. In *Emotional and Ethical Challenges for Field Research in Africa The Story Behind the Findings,* edited by Susan Thomson, An Ansoms, and Jude Murison, 12–26. London: Palgrave Macmillan.

Kalekin-Fishman, Devorah. 2013. 'Sociology of everyday life'. *Current Sociological Review* 61, nos. 5–6: 714–32.

Kalyvas, Stathis. 2004. 'The Urban Bias in Research on Civil Wars'. *Security Studies* 13, no. 3: 160–90.

Kalyvas, Stathis. 2006. *The Logic of Violence in Civil War.* New York: Cambridge University Press.

Kapferrer, Bruce. 1973. 'Social Network and Conjugal Role in Urban Zambia: towards a Reformulation of the Bott Hypothesis'. In *Network Analysis: Studies in Human Interaction,* edited by Jeremy Boissevain and J. Clyde Mitchell, 83–110. The Hague: Mouton.

Kapoor, Ilan. 2004. 'Hyper-Self-Reflexive Development: Spivak on Representing the Third World "Other"'. *Third World Quarterly* 25, no. 4: 627–47.

Keikelame, J. Mpoe. 2018. '"The Tortoise under the Couch": An African Woman's Reflections on Negotiating Insider-Outsider Positionalities and Issues of Serendipity on Conducting a Qualitative Research Project in Cape Town, South Africa'. *International Journal of Social Research Methodology* 21, no. 2: 219–30.

Kesselring, Rita. 2017. *Bodies of Truth: Law, Memory, and Emancipation in Post-Apartheid South Africa.* Stanford: Stanford University Press.

Kobayashi, Audrey. 1994. 'Coloring the Field: Gender, Race, and the Politics of Fieldwork'. *Professional Geographer* 46, no. 1: 73–80.

Kondo, Dorinne. 1986. 'Dissolution and Reconstitution of Self: Implications for Anthropological Epistemology'. *Cultural Anthropology* 1, no. 1: 74–88

Kovats-Bernat, J. Christopher. 2002. 'Negotiating Dangerous Fields: Pragmatic Strategies for Fieldwork amid Violence and Terror'. *American Anthropologist* 104, no. 1: 208–22.

Kuzmits, Bernd. 2008. 'Losing My Illusions. Methodological Dreams and Reality in Local Governance Research in the Amu Darya Borderlands'. In *Fieldwork in Difficult Environments: Methodology as Boundary Work in Development Research,* edited by Caleb Wall and Peter P. Mollinga, 19–42. Berlin: LIT Verlag.

Labov, Willliam. 2010. 'Oral Narratives of Personal Experience'. In *Cambridge Encyclopedia of the Language Sciences,* edited by Patrick Hogan, 546–48. Cambridge: Cambridge University Press.

Lacan, Jacques. 1986. *Le Séminaire,* livre VII, *L'éthique de la psychanalyse.* Paris: Seuil.

Ladson-Billings, Gloria. 2003. '"It's your world, I'm just trying to explain it": Understanding Our Epistemological and Methodological Challenges'. *Qualitative Inquiry* 9, no. 1: 5–12.

Lake, Milli, Samantha Majic, and Rahsaan Maxwell. 2019. *Research on Vulnerable and Marginalized Populations.* February 13. American

Political Science Association Organized Section for Qualitative and Multi-Method Research, Qualitative Transparency Deliberations, Working Group Final Reports, Report IV.3. https://ssrn.com/abstract=3333511. Accessed 8 January 2020.

Landry, Jean-Michel. 2006. 'La Violence symbolique chez Bourdieu'. *Aspects Sociologiques* 13, no. 1: 85–92.

Lawther, Cheryl, Rachel Killean and Lauren Dempster. 2019. 'Working with Others: Reflections on Fieldwork in Postconflict Societies'. *International Journal of Transitional Justice* 13: 387–97.

Le Renard, Améle. 2010. 'Partager des Contraintes de Genre avec les Enquêtées. Quelques Réflexions à Partir du cas Saoudien'. *Genèses* 4, no. 81: 128–41.

Lee, Raymond M. 1993. *Doing Research on Sensitive Topics*. Thousand Oaks: Sage.

Lee-Treweek, Geraldine, and Stephanie Linkogle. 2000. 'Putting Danger in the Frame'. In *Danger in the Field: Risk and Ethics in Social Research*, edited by Geraldine Lee-Treweek and Stephanie Linkogle, 8–25. London: Routledge

Leonardo, Zeus. 2018. 'Dis-orienting Western Knowledge: Coloniality, Curriculum and Crisis'. *The Cambridge Journal of Anthropology* 36, no. 2: 7–20.

Lerum, Kari. 2001. 'Subjects of Desire: Academic Armor, Intimate Ethnography, and the Production of Critical Knowledge'. *Qualitative Inquiry* 7, no. 4: 466–83.

Li, Jun. 2008. 'Ethical Challenges in Participant Observation: A Reflection on Ethnographic Fieldwork'. *The Qualitative Report* 13, no. 1: 100–15.

Lindner, Evelin. 2004. 'Genocide, Humiliation, and Inferiority: an Interdisciplinary Perspective'. In *Genocides by the Oppressed: Subaltern Genocide in Theory and Practice*, edited by Nicholas A. Robins and Adam Jones, 138–58. Bloomington: Indiana University Press.

Lobo-Guerrero, Luis. 2013. 'Wondering as Research Attitude'. In *Research Methods in Critical Security Studies: An Introduction*, edited by Mark B. Salter and Can E. Mutlu, 25–8. London: Routledge.

Lombard, Louisa. 2016. *State of Rebellion: Violence and Intervention in the Central African Republic*. London: Zed Books

Lumumba, Patrick. 2017. 'Magufulification of Africa'. Filmed June 21 2017 in Dar es Salaam, Tanzania. YouTube Video. https://www.youtube.com/watch?v=bVBHQeeZwt4&t=84s. Accessed 19 April 2019.

Macamo, Elísio. 2017. *The Taming of Fate. Approaches to Risk from a Social Action Perspective – Case Studies from Southern Mozambique*. Dakar: CODESRIA.

Macé, Éric. 2015. *L'Après-Patriarcat*. Paris: Seuil.

MacGaffey, Janet, and Rémy Bazenguissa-Ganga. 2000. *Congo-Paris: Transnational Traders on the Margins of the Law*. Bloomington: Indiana University Press.

Mackenzie, Catriona, Christopher McDowell, and Eileen Pittaway. 2007. 'Beyond "Do No Harm": The Challenge of Constructing Ethical Relationships in Refugee Research'. *Journal of Refugee Studies* 20, no. 2: 299–319.

MacLean, Lauren Morris, Elliot Posner, Susan Thomson, and Elisabeth Jean Wood. 2019. *Research Ethics and Human Subjects: A Reflexive Openness Approach* (12 February). American Political Science Association Organized Section for Qualitative and Multi-Method Research, Qualitative Transparency Deliberations, Working Group Final Reports, Report I.2. https://ssrn.com/abstract=3332887. Accessed 8 January 2020.

Madge, Clare. 1993. 'Boundary Disputes: Comments on Sidaway (1992)'. *Area* 25, no. 3: 294– 99.

Madlingozi, Tshepo. 2010. 'On Transitional Justice Entrepreneurs and the Production of Victims'. *Journal of Human Rights Practice* 2, no. 2: 208–28.

Mama, Amina. 2000. 'Why We Must Write: Personal Reflections on Linking the Alchemy of Science with the Relevance of Activism'. *Agenda: Empowering Women for Gender Equity* 46: 13–20.

Manning, Jennifer. 2018. 'Becoming a Decolonial Feminist Ethnographer: Addressing the Complexities of Positionality and Representation'. *Management Learning* 49, no. 3: 1–27.

Martin, Emily. 1991. 'The Egg and the Sperm. How Science has Constructed a Romance Based on Stereotypical Male-Females Roles'. *Journal of Women in Culture and Society* 16, no. 3: 485–501.

Maunier, Sophie. 2017. 'De quelle Épistémologie l'Ethnométhodologie est-elle le Nom?'. *SociologieS*. 13 November.

Mazurana, Dyan, Karen Jacobson, and Lacey Andrews Gale, eds. 2014. *Research Methods in Conflict Settings: A View from Below*. Cambridge: Cambridge University Press.

Mbembe, Achille. 1992. 'The Banality of Power and the Aesthetics of Vulgarity in the Postcolony'. *Public Culture* 4, no. 2: 1–30.

Mbembe, Achille. 2000. *On the Postcolony*. Berkeley: University of California Press.

Mbembe, Achille. 2013. *Critique de la Raison Nègre*. Paris: La Découverte.

McCurdy, Sheryl. 1996. 'Learning the Dance, Initiating Relationships'. In *In Pursuit of History: Fieldwork in Africa*, edited by Carolyn Keyes Adenaike and Jan Vansina, 41–56. Portsmouth: Heinemann.

McLean, Athena and Annette Liebing, eds. 2007. *The Shadow Side of Fieldwork: Exploring the Blurred Borders between Ethnography and Life*. Malden: Blackwell Publishing.

Merriam, Sharan B., Juanita Johnson-Bailey, Ming-Yeh Lee, Youngwha Kee, Gabo Ntseane, and Mazanah Muhamad. 2001. 'Power and Positionality: Negotiating Insider/Outsider Status Within and Across Cultures'. *International Journal of Lifelong Education* 20. no. 5: 405–16.

Mestiri, Soumaya. 2016. *Décoloniser le féminisme: une approche transculturelle*. Paris: Vrin.

Meyer, Scott D. 2007. *From Horror Story to Manageable Risk: Formulating Safety Strategies for Peace Researchers*. Master's thesis, Peace Studies. University of Tromsø, Norway.

Millar, Gearoid. 2018. 'Ethnographic Peace Research: The Underappreciated Benefits of Long-term Fieldwork'. *International Peacekeeping* 25, no. 5: 653–76.

Milligan, Lizzi. 2016. 'Insider-Outsider-Inbetweener? Researcher Positioning, Participative Methods and Cross-Cultural Educational Research'. *Compare: A Journal of Comparative and International Education* 46, no. 2: 235–50.

Mitchell, John C. 1973. 'Network, Norms and Institutions'. In *Network Analysis: Studies in Human Interaction*, edited by Jeremy Boissevain and J. Clyde Mitchell, 83–110. The Hague: Mouton.

Morgan, S. 1983. 'Toward a Politics of "Feelings": Beyond the Dialectic of Thought and Action'. *Women's Studies* 10, no. 2: 203–23.

Moussaoui, Abderrahmane. 2006. *De la Violence en Algérie. Les lois du Chaos*. Arles: Actes Sud.

Mügge, Liza, Celeste Montoya, Akwugo Emejulu, and S. Laurel Weldon. 2018. 'Intersectionality and the Politics of Knowledge Production'. *European Journal of Politics and Gender* 1, no. 1–2: 17–36.

Mullings, Beverley. 1999. 'Insider or Outsider, Both or Neither: Some Dilemmas of Interviewing in a Cross-Cultural Setting'. *Geoforum* 30: 337–50.

Munthali, Alister. 2001. 'Doing Fieldwork at Home: Some Personal Experiences among the Tumbuka of Northern Malawi'. *African Anthropologist* 8, no. 2: 114–36.

Munyakazi, Justin B. 2018. 'Examining the Role of Youth in the Maï-Maï Yakutumba Insurgency'. *Kujenga Amani*. http://kujenga-amani.ssrc.org/2018/02/01/

examining-the-role-of-youth-in-the-mai-mai-yakutumba-insurgency/.
Accessed 5 May 2018.

Neocosmos, Michael. 2010. *From 'Foreign Natives' to 'Native Foreigners'.*
Explaining Xenophobia in Post-apartheid South Africa: Citizenship and
Nationalism, Identity and Politics. Dakar: CODESRIA.

Newbury, Catharine. 1988. *The Cohesion of Oppression: Clientship and*
Ethnicity in Rwanda, 1860–1960. New York: Columbia University Press.

Newbury, David and Catharine Newbury. 2000. 'Bringing the Peasants
Back In: Agrarian Themes in the Construction and Corrosion of Statist
Historiography in Rwanda'. *American Historical Review* 105, no. 3:
832–78.

Nilan, Pamela. 2002. '"Dangerous Fieldwork" Re-Examined: The Question
of Researcher Subject Position'. *Qualitative Research* 2, no. 3: 363–86.

Nolte, Insa. 2019. 'The Future of African Studies: What we can do to keep
Africa at the heart of our research'. *Journal of African Cultural Studies*
31, no. 3: 296–310.

Nordenhaug, Erik and Jack Simmons. 2018. 'The Outsourcing of Ethical
Thinking'. *Journal of Human Values* 24, no. 2: 1–12.

Nordstrom, Carolyn. 1995. 'War on the Front Lines'. In *Fieldwork under*
Fire: Contemporary Studies of Violence and Survival, edited by Carolyn
Nordstrom and Antonius Robben, 129–54. Berkeley: University of Cal-
ifornia Press.

Nordstrom, Carolyn and Antonius C.G.M Robben, eds. 1995. *Fieldwork*
under Fire: Contemporary Studies of Violence and Survival. Berkeley:
University of California Press.

Norman, Julie. 2009. 'Got Trust? The Challenge of Gaining Access in
Conflict Zones'. In *Surviving Field Research: Working in Violent and Dif-*
ficult Situations, edited by Chandra Lekha Sriram, John C. King, Julie
A. Mertus, Olga Martin-Ortega, and Joanna Herman 71–90. London:
Routledge.

Nyenyezi Bisoka, Aymar. 2016a. 'Accéder aux 'Discours Cachés' aux Élites
au Pouvoir'. In *Eprouver l'altérité,* edited by Clémentine Gutron and
Vincent Legrand, 33–52. Louvain: Presses Universitaires de Louvain.

Nyenyezi Bisoka, Aymar. 2016b. *Invention de la terre et production des*
anormaux dans le dispositif foncier en Afrique. Pouvoir et résistance à
l'accaparement des terres en Afrique des Grands Lacs. PhD dissertation,
Université catholique de Louvain, 2016.

Nyenyezi Bisoka, Aymar. 2017. 'Accéder aux "discours caches" des élites
dominantes: défis éthiques et épistémologiques liés à la perception
des rôles et du statut du chercheur'. In *Défis de la recherche de terrain,*

edited by Clémentine Gutron, Vincent Legrand and An Ansoms, 33–52. Louvain: Presses Universitaires de Louvain.

Nyenyezi Bisoka, Aymar, An Ansoms, and Emery Mushagalusa Mudinga. 2017. 'Transgression des règles dans la gestion foncière au Burundi : la cathégorie locale en question'. In *Anthropologie des prédations foncières. Entreprises minières et pouvoir locaux*, edited by Michèle G. Leclerc-Olive, 85–98. Paris: Éditions des Archives contemporaines.

Nzongola-Ntalaja, Georges. 2002. *The Congo: From Leopold to Kabila: A People's History*. New York: Zed Books.

O'Donoghue, Kate. 2015. 'Sovereign Exception: Notes on the Thought of Giorgio Agamben'. *Critical Legal Thinking*. 2 July. http://critical-legalthinking.com/2015/07/02/sovereign-exception-notes-on-the-thought-of-giorgio-agamben/. Accessed 9 September 2015.

Ochonu, E. Moses. 2019. 'Racism or Classism? Africa's Hidden Race Problem'. *The Republic* 3, no. 1. https://www.republic.com.ng/vol3-no1/racism-or-classism/. Accessed 28 September 2019.

Ouattara, Fatoumata. 2004. 'Une Étrange Familiarité. Les Exigences de l'Anthropologie "Chez Soi"'. *Cahiers d'Études Africaines* 3, no. 175: 635–58.

Owen, Joy. 2011. *'On se debrouille:' Congolese Migrants' Search for Survival and Success in Muizenberg, Cape Town*. PhD dissertation, Department of Social Anthropology, Rhodes University, South Africa.

Owen, Joy. 2015. *Congolese Social Networks: Living on the Margins in Muizenberg, Cape Town*. Lanham: Lexington Books.

Owen-Smith, Jason and Walter W. Powell. 2004. 'Knowledge Networks as Channels and Conduits: The Effects of Spillovers in the Boston Biotechnology Community'. *Organization Science* 15, no. 1: 5–21.

Owor Ogora, Lino. 2013. 'The Contested Fruits of Research in War-Torn Countries: My Insider Experience in Northern Uganda'. In *Emotional and Ethical Challenges for Field Research in Africa: The Story Behind the Findings*, edited by Susan Thomson, An Ansoms, and Jude Murison, 27–41. London: Palgrave Macmillan.

Parkinson, Sarah. 2019. 'The Dignity of Complexity: Being Human in Political Science'. *Qualitative and Mixed Methods Research* 16, no. 1: 39–41.

Peritore, N. Patrick. 1990. 'Reflections on Dangerous Fieldwork'. *American Sociologist* 21, no. 4: 359–72.

Perks, Robert and Alistair Thomson, eds. 1998. *The Oral History Reader*. London: Routledge.

Piper, Heather. and Helen Simons. 2005. 'Ethical Responsibility in Social Research'. In *Research Methods in the Social Sciences*, edited by Chava

Frankfort-Nachmias, David Nachmias and Jack DeWaard, 56–63. New York: Worth Publishers.

Pongo, Martin Kalulambi. 1997. *Etre Luba au XXe Siècle: Identité Chrétienne et Ethnicité au Congo-Kinshasa*. Paris: Karthala Editions.

Powell, Walter W., Kenneth Koput, and Laurel Smith-Doerr. 1996. 'Interorganizational Collaboration and the Locus of Innovation: Networks of Learning in Biotechnology'. *Administrative Science Quarterly* 41, no. 1: 116–45.

Pratt, Mary Louise. 1994. 'Transculturation and Autoethnography: Peru, 1615/1980'. In *Colonial Discourse/Postcolonial Theory*, edited by Francis Barker, Peter Hulme and Margaret Iverson, 24–46. Manchester: Manchester University Press.

Probst, Barbara. 2015. 'The Eye Regards Itself: Benefits and Challenges of Reflexivity in Qualitative Social Work Research'. *Social Work Research* 39, no. 1: 37–48.

Prunier, Gérard. 2011. *Africa's World War: Congo, the Rwandan Genocide, and the Making of a Continental Catastrophe*. Oxford: Oxford University Press.

Pugh, Sarah. 2014. 'Human Mobility in South Africa'. In *Africans on the Move: Human Mobility in Ghana, Nigeria, Angola and South Africa*, edited by Fabio Baggio, 161–95. Cape Town: Scalabrini Institute for Human Mobility in Africa.

Pulido, Laura, 2008. 'FAQs: Frequently (Un)Asked Questions about Being a Scholar Activist'. In *Engaging Contradictions: Theory, Politics and Methods of Activist Scholarship*, edited by Charles Hale, 341–66. Berkeley: University of California Press.

Quivy, Raymond, and Luc Van Campenhoudt. 2011. *Manuel de recherches en sciences sociales*, fourth edition. Paris: Dunod.

Reed-Danahay, Deborah. 1997. 'Introduction'. In *Auto/ethnography: Rewriting the Self and Social*, edited by Deborah Reed-Danahay, 1–20. Oxford: Berg.

Reinharz, Shulamit. 1992. *Feminist Methods in Social Research*. New York: Oxford University Press.

Rémy, Catherine. 2014. *Accepter de se Perdre. Les Leçons Ethnographiques de Jeanne Favret-Saada. SociologieS*. 24 June.

Reyntjens, Filip. 2009. *Les risques du métier. Trois décennies de 'chercheur-acteur' au Rwanda et au Burundi*. Paris: L'Harmattan.

Reyntjens, Filip. 2010. *The Great African War: Congo and Regional Geopolitics, 1996–2006*. Cambridge: Cambridge University Press.

Robben, Antonius. 1995. 'The Politics of Truth and Emotion among Victims'. In *Fieldwork under Fire: Contemporary Studies of Violence and*

Survival, edited by Carolyn Nordstrom and Antonius Robben, 81–104. Berkeley: University of California Press.

Robben, Antonius C.G.M. and Jeffrey A. Sluka. 2012. *Ethnographic Fieldwork: An Anthropological Reader,* 2nd edition. Malden: Wiley-Blackwell.

Robinson, Fiona. 2011. 'Stop Talking and Listen: Discourse Ethics and Feminist Care Ethics in International Political Theory'. *Millennium: Journal of International Studies* 39, no. 3: 845–60.

Rose, Gillian. 1997. 'Situating Knowledges: Positionality, Reflexivities and Other Tactics'. *Progress in Human Geography* 21, no. 3: 305–20.

Roxburgh, Shelagh. 2017. 'Read Black and White: Decolonizing African Studies in North America'. Working Paper Series, Conflict in Difficult Settings Website. http://conflictfieldresearch.colgate.edu/wp-content/uploads/2017/07/Read-Black-and-White-Decolonizing-African-studies.pdf. Accessed 19 August 2017.

Roy, Arundhati. 2004. 'Peace and the New Corporate Liberation Theology'. *The 2004 Sydney Peace Prize Lecture.* http://sydney.edu.au/news/84.html?newsstoryid=279. Accessed 12 September 2019.

Rutazibwa, Olivia U. 2018. 'Epistemic Diversity: Understanding epistemic diversity'. *International Institute of Social Studies.* July 4. https://www.iss.nl/en/news/epistemic-diversity-i-understanding-epistemic-diversity. Accessed 14 June 2019.

Ryan, Louise and Magdolna Lőrinc. 2016. '"Getting your foot in the door": The Role of Serendipity, Heightened Sensitivity and Social Networks in Recruiting Education Research Participants'. *1st International Symposium on Qualitative Research, CIAIQ,* 5: 87–96.

Sabourin, Paul. 1997. 'Perspective sur la Mémoire Sociale de Maurice Halbwachs'. *Sociologie et Sociétés* 29, no. 2: 139–61.

Said, Edward. 2000. *Reflections on Exile.* Cambridge: Harvard University Press.

Sanford, Victoria. 2006. 'Excavations of the Heart. Reflections on Truth, Memory and Structures of Understanding'. In *Engaged Observer. Anthropology, Advocacy and Activism,* edited by Victoria Sanford and Asale Angel-Ajani, 19–41. Princeton: Rutgers University Press.

Sangarasivam, Yamuna. 2001. 'Researcher, Informant, "Assassin", Me'. *Geographical Review* 91, no. 1: 95–104.

Sayigh, Rosemary. 1998. 'Palestinian Camp Women as Tellers of History'. *Journal of Palestine Studies* 27, no 2: 42–58.

Scarry, Elaine. 1985. *The Body in Pain: The Making and Unmaking of the World.* Oxford: Oxford University Press.

Scheper-Hughes, Nancy. 1993. *Death Without Weeping: The Violence of Everyday Life in Brazil.* Berkeley: University of California Press.

Scheper-Hughes, Nancy. 2004. 'Undoing: Social Suffering and Politics of Remorse in the New South Africa'. In *Violence in War and Peace: An Anthology*, edited by Nancy Scheper-Hughes and Philippe Bourgois. Malden, MA: Blackwell Publishing.

Schrag, Zachary, ed. 2006. *The Institutional Review Blog: News and Commentary about Institutional Review Board Oversight of the Humanities and Social Sciences.* http://www.institutionalreviewblog.com/2006/. Accessed 9 May 2019.

Schrag, Zachary. 2010. *Ethical Imperialism: Institutional Review Boards and the Social Sciences, 1965–2009.* Baltimore: Johns Hopkins University Press.

Schulz, Philipp. 2018. 'The "Ethical Loneliness" of Male Sexual Violence Survivors in Northern Uganda: Gendered Reflections on Silencing'. *International Feminist Journal of Politics* 20, no. 4: 583–601

Schwartz-Shea, Peregrine. 2006. 'Judging Quality: Evaluative Criteria and Epistemic Communities'. In *Interpretation and Method: Empirical Research Methods and the Interpretative Turn*, 2nd edition, edited by Dvora Yanow and Peregrine Schwartz-Shea, 89–113. Armonk: M.E. Sharpe Press.

Scott, James C. 1990. *Domination and the Arts of Resistance: Hidden Transcripts.* New Haven, CT: Yale University Press.

Shamy, Soheir. 1988. 'Fieldwork in my Egyptian Homeland'. In *Arab Women in the Field: Studying Your Own Society*, edited by Soraya Altorki and Camillia Fawzi El-Solh, 69–90. Syracuse: Syracuse University Press.

Shesterinina, Anastasia. 2018. 'Ethics, Empathy, and Fear in Research on Violent Conflict'. *Journal of Peace Research* 56, no. 2: 1–13.

Simon, Herbert Alexander. 1979. *Models of Thought.* New Haven, CT: Yale University Press.

Skjelsbaek, Inger. 2018. 'Silence Breakers in War and Peace: Research on Gender and Violence with an Ethics of Engagement'. *Social Politics* 25, no. 4: 496–520.

Sluka, Jeffrey A. 1995. 'Reflections on Managing Danger in Fieldwork: Dangerous Anthropology in Belfast'. In *Fieldwork under Fire: Contemporary Studies of Violence and Survival*, edited by Carolyn Nordstrom and Antonius C.M.G. Robben, 276–94. Berkeley: University of California Press.

Sluka, Jeffrey A. 2009. 'The Contribution of Anthropology to Critical Terrorism Studies'. In *Critical Terrorism Studies: A New Research Agenda*, edited by Richard Jackson, Marie Breen Smyth, and Joeren Gunning, 138–55. London and New York: Routledge.

Smith, Linda Tuhiwai. 2012. *Decolonizing Methodologies: Research and Indigenous Peoples*, 2nd edition. London: Zed Books.

Smyth, Marie and Gillian Robinson, eds. 2001. *Researching Violently Divided Societies: Ethical and Methodological Issues*. Tokyo: United Nations Press.

Spivak, Gayatri Chakravorty. 1993. 'Can the Subaltern Speak?'. In *Colonial Discourse and Post-Colonial Theory: A Reader*, edited by Paul Williams and Laura Crisman, 66–111. New York: Columbia University Press.

Sriram, Chandra Lekha. 2009. 'Maintenance of Standards of Protection during Writeup and Publication'. In *Surviving Field Research: Working in Violent and Difficult Situations*, edited by Chandra Lekha. Sriram, John C. King, Julie Mertus, Olga Martín-Ortega, and Johanna Herman, 57–67. London: Routledge.

Sriram, Chandra Lekha, John C. King, Julie A. Mertus, Olga Martín-Ortega and Johanna Herman, eds. 2009. *Surviving Field Research: Working in Violent and Difficult Situations*. London: Routledge.

Steinberg, Jonny. 2005. *A Mixed Reception: Mozambican and Congolese Refugees in South Africa*. Pretoria: Institute for Security Studies.

Stern, Maria. 2006. 'Racism, Sexism, Classism and Much More: Reading Security-identity in Marginalized Sites'. In *Feminist Methodologies for International Relations*, edited by Brooke A. Ackerly, Maria Stern, and Jacqui True, 174–97. Cambridge: Cambridge University Press.

Straus, Scott. 2004. 'How Many Perpetrators Were There in the Rwandan Genocide: An Estimate'. *Journal of Genocide Research* 6, no. 1: 85–98.

Straus, Scott. 2015. *Making and Unmaking Nations: War, Leadership, and Genocide in Modern Africa*. Ithaca: Cornell University Press.

Suzuki, Daiyu and Edwin Mayorga. 2014. 'Scholar-Activism: A Twice-Told Tale'. *Multicultural Perspectives* 16, no. 1: 16–20.

Taylor, Jodie. 2011. 'The Intimate Insider: Negotiating the Ethics of Friendship when doing Insider Research'. *Qualitative Research* 11, no. 1: 3–22.

Thaler, Kai M. 2019. 'Reflexivity and Temporality in Researching Violent Settings: Problems with the Replicability and Transparency Regime'. *Geopolitics* DOI: 10.1080/14650045.2019.1643721.

Theidon, Kimberley. 2014. *'How was your trip?' Self-care for Researchers Working and Writing on Violence*. Social Science Research Council, Drugs, Security and Democracy Program, DSD Working Papers on Research Security: No. 2. http://webarchive.ssrc.org/working-papers/DSD_ResearchSecurity_02_Theidon.pdf. Accessed 9 July 2020.

Thomson, Susan M. 2009a. '"That is not what we authorised you to do...": Access and Government Interference in Highly Politicised Research Environments'. In *Surviving Field Research: Working in Violent and*

Difficult Situations, edited by Chandra Lekha Sriram, John C. King, Julie A. Mertus, Olga Martin-Ortega, and Johanna Herman, 108– 24. London: Routledge.

Thomson, Susan. 2009b. *Developing Ethical Guidelines for Researchers Working in Post-Conflict Environments.* Research Report, Program on States and Security, City University of New York. http://conflictfieldresearch.colgate.edu/wp content/uploads/2015/02/Developing-Ethical-Guidelines.pdf. Accessed 25 February 2020.

Thomson Susan. 2010. 'Getting Close to Rwandans since the Genocide: Studying Everyday Life in Highly Politicized Research Settings'. *African Studies Review* 53 no. 3: 19–34.

Thomson, Susan. 2011. 'Re-education for Reconciliation: Participant Observations on *Ingando*'. In *Reconstructing Rwanda: State Building and Human Rights after Mass Violence,* edited by Scott Straus and Lars Waldorf, 331–39. Madison: University of Wisconsin Press.

Thomson, Susan. 2013a. *Whispering Truth to Power: Resistance to Reconciliation in Postgenocide Rwanda.* Madison: University of Wisconsin Press.

Thomson, Susan. 2013b. 'Academic Integrity and Ethical Responsibilities in Post-Genocide Rwanda: Working with Research Ethics Boards to Prepare for Fieldwork with "Human Subjects"'. In *Emotional and Ethical Challenges for Field Research in Africa: The Story Behind the Findings,* edited by Susan Thomson, An Ansoms, and Jude Murison, 139–54. London: Palgrave Macmillan.

Thomson, Susan. 2013c. 'Agency as Silence and Muted Voice: The Problem-solving Networks of Unaccompanied Somali Refugee Girls in Eastleigh, Nairobi'. *Conflict, Security and Development* 13, no. 5: 589–609.

Thomson, Susan. 2017. 'The Long Shadow of Genocide in Rwanda'. *Current History* 116, no. 790: 183–88.

Thomson, Susan. 2018a. *Rwanda: From Genocide to Precarious Peace.* New Haven and London: Yale University Press.

Thomson, Susan. 2018b. 'Engaged Silences as Political Agency in Postgenocide Rwanda: Jeanne's Story'. In *Gendered Silences in Contested Terrains,* edited by Swati Parashar and Jane Parpart, 110–23. London: Routledge.

Thomson, Susan. 2020. 'Settler Genocide in Rwanda? Colonial Legacies of Everyday Violence'. In *Settler Colonialism and Genocide: Reflections on the Role of Civilians in Driving Exterminatory Violence,* edited by Mohamed Adhikari, 241–65. Cape Town: University of Cape Town Press.

Thomson, Susan, An Ansoms, and Jude Murison, eds. 2013. *Emotional and Ethical Challenges for Field Research in Africa The Story Behind the Findings.* London: Palgrave MacMillan.

Tolich, Martin. 2004. 'Internal Confidentiality: When Confidentiality Assurances Fail Relational Informants'. *Qualitative Sociology* 27, no. 1: 101–6.

United States Department of Health and Human Services. 1979. *The Belmont Report: Ethical Principles and Guidelines for the Protection of Human* Subjects. https://www.hhs.gov/ohrp/regulations-and-policy/belmont-report/index.html. Accessed 19 January 2017.

Unluer, Sema. 2012. 'Being an Insider Researcher while conducting Case Study Research'. *Qualitative Report* 17, no 29: 1–14.

Uzzi, Brian. 1996. 'The Sources and Consequences of Embeddedness for the Economic Performance of Organizations: The Network Effect'. *American Sociological Revue* 61, no. 4: 674–98.

Vansina, Jan. 1985. *Oral Tradition as History.* Madison: University of Wisconsin Press.

Vorrath, Judith. 2013. 'Challenges of Interviewing political Elites: A View from the Top in Post-War Burundi'. In *Emotional and Ethical Challenges for Field Research in Africa The Story Behind the Findings,* edited by Susan Thomson, An Ansoms and Jude Murison, 57–69. London: Palgrave Macmillan

Vuninga, Rosette Sifa. 2014. *Théâtres and mikilistes: Congolese films and Congolese diasporic identity in the Post-Mobutu period (1998–2011).* MA dissertation, History Department, University of the Western Cape.

Vuninga, Rosette Sifa. 2017. *Combattants: Activists or Criminals? A Reflection on Ethnoregionalism and Political Violence among Congolese Immigrants in South Africa.* Kujenga Amani. http://forums.ssrc.org/kujenga-amani/2017/03/14/Combattants-activists-or-criminals-a-reflection-on-ethnoregionalism-and-political-violence-among-congolese-immigrants-in-south-africa/#.WQO7styxWM9. Accessed 29 April 2017.

Wainaina, Binyavanga. 2006. 'How to Write about Africa'. *Granta 92: The View from Africa.* 19 January. https://granta.com/how-to-write-about-africa/. Accessed 21 June 2019.

Wall, Caleb R.L and Peter P. Mollinga, eds. 2008. *Fieldwork in Difficult Environments: Methodology as Boundary Work in Development Research.* Berlin: LIT Verlag.

Wali, Farhaan. 2018. 'An Oral History Approach to Post-conflict Identity in Bosnia and Herzegovina'. *Oral History* 46, no. 1: 67–77.

Wamai, Njoki. 2014. 'First Contact with the Field: Experiences of an Early Career Researcher in the Context of National and International Politics in Kenya'. *Journal of Human Rights Practice* 6, no. 2: 213–22.

Warr, Deborah J. 2004. 'Stories in the Flesh and Voices in the Head: Reflections on the Context and Impact of Research with Disadvantaged Populations'. *Qualitative Health Research* 14, no. 4: 578–87.

White, Luise. 2000. *Speaking with Vampires: Rumor and History in Colonial Africa*. Berkeley: University of California Press.

Wilson, Shawn. 2008. *Research is Ceremony: Indigenous Research Methods*. Black Point: Fernwood Publishing.

Wood, Elisabeth Jean. 2006. 'The Ethical Challenges of Field Research in Conflict Zones'. *Qualitative Sociology* 29, no. 3: 373–86.

Wood, Elisabeth J. 2013. 'Reflections on the Challenges, Dilemmas, and Rewards of Research in Conflict Zones'. In *Research Methods in Conflict Settings: A View from Below*, edited by Dyan Mazurana, Karen Jacobsen, and Lacey Andrews Gale, 295–308. Cambridge: Cambridge University Press.

Wylie, Alison. 2003. 'Why Standpoint Matters'. In *Science and Other Cultures: Issues in Philosophies of Science and Technology*, edited by Robert Figueroa and Sandra G. Harding, 26–48. London: Routledge.

Yacob-Haliso, Olajumoke. 2019. 'Intersectionalities and Access in Fieldwork in Postconflict Liberia: Motherland, Motherhood, and Minefields'. *African Affairs* 118, no. 470: 168–81.

Yanow, Dvora. 2009. 'Dear Author, Dear Reader: The Third Hermeneutic in Writing and Reviewing Ethnography'. In *Political Ethnography: What Immersion Contributes to the Study of Power*, edited by Edward Schatz, 275–302. Chicago: University of Chicago Press.

Yanow, Dvora and Peregrine Schwartz-Shea. 2008. 'Reforming Institutional Board Policy: Issues in Implementation and Field Research'. *PS: Political Science & Politics* 41, no. 3: 483–94.

Yanow, Dvora and Peregrine Schwartz-Shea. 2016. 'Encountering your IRB 2.0: What Political Scientists Need to Know'. *PS: Political Science & Politics* 49, no. 2: 277–86.

Young, Iris Marion. 2004. 'Five faces of oppression'. In *Oppression, Privilege, & Resistance: Theoretical Perspectives of Racism, Sexism and Heterosexism*, edited by Lisa Heldke and P. O'Connor, 37–62. Boston: McGraw Hill.

Zeilig, Leo. 2015. *Lumumba: Africa's Lost Leader*. London: Haus Publishing.

Zevallos, Zuleyka. 2017. 'Protecting Activist Academics Against Public Harassment'. *The Other Sociologist*. 6 July. https://othersociologist. com/2017/07/06/activist-academics-public-harassment. Accessed 20 June 2019.

Index